Melchizedek ..

DR. KLUANE

A NEW Order   6

    Much to Say – Hard to Understand   11
    Meat   12
    Abram and Melchizedek   15
    A Name – A SEED!   17
    Hebrew   19
    Two Kinds Of Seeds   19

A KING   23

    Melchizedek Was The King Of Righteousness   25
    Tzedek is the Melchizedek Rule   26
    Prosperity   27
    The War   40
    The Convergence   43
    The Rescue   45

Priesthood of Melchizedek   47

    El Elyon   48
    Communion   49
    Victory of Communion   50
    The BLESSING   52
    Possessor of Heaven and Earth   55
    The Decision   56
    How the Priesthood Changed   61

Old Testament Priesthood   62
"Another of a Different Kind" Comes by Necessity!"   67
Melchizedek Was The First Priesthood And The Last!   68
Jesus Is BETTER   69
An Oath   71
Moving Forward   71

Identity of Melchizedek   76

Without Genealogy   78
Theopany   80
Why Melchizedek Could Have Been Be Jesus   81
Not a Theopany   83
Interesting Shem Connection   85
1st or 3rd?   88
After the Flood   90
Jerusalem   92
Moreh   93
Jerusalem   95
Why Shem May Not Have Been Melchizedek: 96

Tithing   97

Principle of Firstborn First-fruit   98
The First Fruit   99
Principle of the SECOND   100
Second Son Jesus   101
Tithing   102
Who Received the Tithe?   103
During The Law   103
School Master   104
Free From the Law   105
The CURSE of the Law   108
WHY?   109
Wrong Ways   113
Should We Tithe?   114
Melchizedek Giving   115
New Testament Giving   116
A Change   119
So... Now What?   121
Giving UP!   122
Is it Okay for Ministers to be Paid?   124

>   The Connection Between Tithing And Communion   125

Imputed Tzedek   126

>   Romans 10:4 - The Righteous of FAITH   134
>   Romans 10:5 -135
>   Righteousness & Glory   138
>   Righteousness Expanded   138
>   Righteous Judgement   140

King of Peace   142

>   Peace Is the Emotion of Faith   144
>   King of Salem   147
>   The Vehicle of Melchizedek Wholeness   148
>   Righteous and Peace Dwell Together   149
>   Trees of RIGHTEOUSNESS   149
>   PEACE is the Fruit   150
>   They Kiss   152
>   Magi (Plural of Latin magus; Greek magoi)   156
>   Zadok - Tzadok The Keepers of the Covenant   158
>   Jesus The Zadok   160

The Keys to Heaven and Earth   165

>   You are BOTH King and Priest   167
>   KING-PRIESTS See The Whole Picture!   176
>   Using Both Sides   180
>   David had the Key   183
>   David was a King   184
>   How Did David Get This Revelation of the King/Priest and Melchizedek?   187
>   The Key of David – Eliakim   188
>   What Was David's KEY?   190
>   The Tabernacle Of David   191
>   Quickened & Endless Life   199
>   The Power of His Endless   201

Bibliography   207

ENDNOTES: 209

Dear Reader,

The Bible book of Hebrews says that learning about Melchizedek is "not easy!" That's because this topic is meat and not milk! And that's also why this book gives you a lot of background pieces about related subjects! And... that's why, before you begin, you know that this study about Melchizedek will not be "easy."

Scripture is often like a gigantic mosaic with strangely unrelated concepts – but as we combine them, they begin to make sense (the ingathering of the Word). The fragments of the body that was broken come together like a giant Three Dimensional (3-D) puzzle.

You can examine one puzzle piece and not see the full picture – you have to build it piece by piece until everything is in place. Sometimes, you have to pick up old discarded pieces and examine them again from another angle.

And... we need an actual copy of the picture to see how it is supposed to look – that comes by revelation. We look again and find a new placement for the missing next piece – and soon we see how each piece fits together to make a greater composite whole than we've known before.

Bear with me as we wade through some of this information. It may seem a little convoluted as we go along – and some concepts and terms are repeated in order to answer each topic.

Each piece is important – even if you think you already know about it! Hopefully, when they fit in this new way, you will gain all new revelation and ideas. That's my prayer!

Dr. Kluane

Introduction

Firstly, let's agree that the Bible is sacred, inerrant, holy, unquestionable and infallible Word of God. What is important to this study about Melchizedek is to understand WHAT was God's Holy intention when written. Firstly, we look to the Holy Spirit, Who is our teacher.

We also look at history to try to discover what the author meant to say with the words used – and how the people understood those words at the time it was written.

The Bible was first translated from the Greek into English 500 years ago. There were many early translations, and many translation errors.

In the 1600s, King James ordered the translators to guarantee that his new version would confirm and reflect the episcopal structure of the Church of England. 47 scholars, all of whom were members of the Church of England, translated according to their perceptions of what they thought would please the King. Unfortunately, the King James Version often arbitrarily leaves out words and sentences and adds others.

The problem is that many MISTAKEN IDEAS from some of these older translations have survived. ideas about SUFFERING and CONDEMNATION, sin consciousness, guilt, and fear. Even now, many of our doctrines and traditions come from these many mistranslated ideas.

But, just as Daniel promised, the BOOKS are OPENING, and we find the NEWNESS of the Holy Word that is fresh every morning!

New Papyrus

Today's believers are most fortunate because we have access to more accurate Scriptural understanding than ever before. In the last 20 years, we have unfolding new evidence from these ANCIENT PAPRIUS that give us supplemental information as to the intended meanings of New Testament words.

- Many of these historical papyri contain an abundant use of the words that only appear a few times in the NT.

- Thanks to abundant historical records from Biblical times (like court documents and so on), we can better understand what these words meant to the people at that time.

Most concordances and commentaries do not include these new findings that have recently come to light. Yes... they were written by well intentioned people. But, they translated the Bible according to their previous perceptions of what they have heard for centuries.

We mention all this because the study of Melchizedek priesthood is impacted by new findings and how that relates to us as individuals. (We will use the name Abram and Abraham interchangeably.)

One of our main topics in this study is RIGHTEOUSNESS. Even as late as this last century, many believers viewed God as a stern and vindictive Ruler Who exhibited meticulous moral wrath against all manner of abominations, deviation, and sin. This Hebrew God focused on having a people "separated" from anything that would detract from living His strict laws of virtue and penance - to the letter! (i.e. Lev 20:22).

> Legalism focuses on increasingly precise punishments for not being righteous and for disobedience (for example Deut 24:1-2, etc.) Burdensomely, their hope of ever achieving individual righteousness rested solely upon the strict obedience of each individual.

> It was believed that if they lived unworthily, their ruthless God would punish them and show no favor to them. This legalistic and fearful lifestyle led to barrenness – and righteousness was never fully discovered.
>
> This conception of a fierce and demanding God profoundly influenced the later Bible translations.

As we search for Melchizedek, it is not to criticize the past. but to learn from it and then move forward valuing the past renewals that brought us here to a fabulous new day. Advancing truth values right principles of past while moving forward to greater Biblical awakening.

But... be prepared! Because we will talk about a lot of Scripture, but also about some legends, beliefs, and other extra-Biblical accounts of the past. OF course these other studies are not equal to Scripture. But, it helps us to understand the thinking of that day and how they understood these same concepts.

You will discover that righteousness is yours and it produces great blessings!

> Hosea 10:12 tells them, *"Sow for yourselves RIGHTEOUSNESS; reap kindness; break up your fallow ground, for it is the time to seek Yahweh, until he comes and rains RIGHTEOUSNESS upon you."*

The New Order

Melchizedek is the New Order!

Much truth was lost in the Dark Ages and Middle Ages. We are still dealing with these old mentalities, ineffective ritual, superstition, and limiting ideas that restrain and hinder destiny. Reformation and change continues.

Wisdom never camps at the doorstep of past rigid obsolete doctrines or embraces ineffective Denominational & doctrinal biases.

The Message BiblE explains it this way, "Under this (*old*) system, the gifts and sacrifices can't really get to the heart of the matter, can't assuage the conscience of the people, but are limited to matters of ritual and behavior. It's essentially a temporary arrangement until a complete overhaul could be made. They are only a matter of food and drink and various ceremonial washings-external regulations applying until the **TIME** of the **NEW ORDER**" (Heb. 9:10, NKJ).

> TIME (kairos) OF THE NEW ORDER. = *diorthosis* straighten thoroughly; rectification, i.e. (specially) like a chiropractor - a new alignment of restoration.
>
> Now is the time for us to be aware of this New Order and the fullness of PROCEEDING TRUTH!

We must not continue like blind Bartamaus, still listening to the same old thinking that has been taught for centuries. HEAR THE SHIFT - God is blowing the whistle and gathering a people unto Himself. This is a new ORDER and a new season of hearing His voice.

Jesus introduced this NEW ORDER when He rose from the dead and gave us His royal priesthood of Melchizedek! ALL WE NEED TO DO is realize what is already ours and BRING it FORWARD.

You and I are handpicked to live and to lead in this hour of the NEW ORDER! Here we stand at the fullness of time. It is the brink of the dawn of a new Day! Melchizedek teachings BRING apostolic order that usher forth greater LIFE. It is an order of wisdom, knowledge, and stability. Truth manifests with increased new relevance!

A NEW Order

"Therefore if any person (all genders, races, classes) be in Christ, he is a new creature: old things (original or primeval) are passed away (totally gone); behold (look and perceive), ALL THINGS (everything) are become (come into existence) NEW" (2 Cor. 5:17).

> "OLD THINGS" are in the past and not fresh. Poor perception, wrong perspective.
>
> NEW is *the word kainos*, which means a freshness or re-freshing. This is not just a noun but a verb - it is the ACT of formation, of a new kind, one that is an unprecedented, novel, uncommon, and unheard of creation.
>
> "IF YOU ARE IN CHRIST, YOU ARE A re-FRESHing to everything around you! So repent (change your mind and purpose); turn around and return [to God], that your sins may be erased (blotted out, wiped clean), that times of re-FRESHing (of recovering from the effects of heat, of reviving with fresh air) may come from the PRESENCE of the Lord" (Acts 3:19 AMP expanded).
>
> Christ is the activator; you are the refreshed newness!

Sight

Your perception changes as you move into this NEW ORDER! At last you can leave the old limited perspectives!

Now, in this New Order, your perception should supersede all previous experiences.

You can see this moving to new fresh way of seeing like when Ezekiel tells about "... a WHEEL in the MIDDLE of a WHEEL... their rings were full of EYES ROUND ABOUT them four." (Ez. 1:15-18). This movement of vision presents new perspectives. The eyes knew wherever the Spirit wanted to go, and they went together. It is no longer just a linear sight. All perspectives are on that wheel.

Stand now where it is fresh and new! Stand behind the Mercy seat (priest's position) look outward across the courtyard. Your view from mercy seat connects as you see from the other (back) side of the cross. Behold, you are in union, one with the Father's eyes. There is NO Veil, there is NO division, there is NO separation. The Holy of Holies and the Holy Place and the Outer Court are now ONE.

Beyond your previous years, you see into new perspectives. You can be like John when he said, "And I SAW a new heaven and a new earth" (Rev 21:1). What do you SEE?

You must EXPECT TO SEE a new heaven and a new earth before there will BE a new heaven and a new earth. You must perceive the imperative of the Melchizedek Priesthood before it becomes a reality!

Creation

We've read the Scriptures multiple times and still they still continue to expand in meaning. The apostolic mandate of the Garden was clear: "Be Fruitful, Multiply, Fill the earth, Subdue, and have Dominion." This cultural mandate reproduces who God is in you!

DOMINION: God said let "them (pl) HAVE dominion." Where? "OVER THE EARTH." (Notice that This command is about EARTH!) Furthermore, it does not say, "Let them TAKE dominion." Dominion is the attribute we HAVE been given as the "power of attorney" to act on God's behalf.

This assignment of the first couple was to initiate the establishment of human rule over the Garden (Kingdom of God) on earth as it is in heaven.

God never changed His mind. Ruling in dominion is still His plan. But, most believers today are not aware of their dominion assignment. You are created to have dominion rule. DOMINION (*radah*) "to cultivate, guard, steward, manage this earth" for the sake of God and of the creation itself.

The purpose of 'radah' is:

- To give humans rulership DOMINON OVER the earth -- NOT other people.

To release God's tangible reality upon the earth.

The Hebrew word for "dominion" comes from the word *basileia* which means TO RULE OR BE KINGLY! Dominion means to rule as the sovereign ruler over the designated territory the Lord gives you.

These first humans were given the PRIESTLY rule (walking and talking with God) and the KINGLY rule as entrusted guardians and stewards of the Paradise Garden.

In the Fall, we see that much was lost. They had never comprehended death, but it happened. They *forgot* that they were given the ability to govern themselves and they lost their Kingdom. Their eyes were closed to their authority (*exousia*, the right to use God's power) to govern this earth.[1]

> In case you think that the commanded blessing of dominion was lost in the Fall, notice that NOAH was also given the same dominion mandate (Gen. 9:1-17). Noah was God's mouthpiece (priestly) to warn of disaster and he worked (kingly) to gather the animals into the ark.
>
> Humanity still had the capacity to rule, they just didn't PERCEIVE it. They inherited forgetfulness, disorder, and chaos.
>
> The influence of a King/Priest is to take ascendency over all that opposes God, and to govern over his own specific territory in order to bring forth the nature, character, culture, and purposes of God.

Summary:

From the beginning of creation, God's INTENTION and PURPOSE was to use human beings to expand His Kingdom upon this earth. In fact, the Kingdom belonged to us in God's mind even before the earth was formed.

> From the beginning, dominion (kingly rule) over this earth was given to humanity in order to bring the Kingdom of heaven to earth! God never changed His mind!

"Come, you who are blessed... inherit the Kingdom prepared for you *from the creation of the world*" (Mat. 25:34). Your Divine Melchizedek Priesthood, gives you the ability to reconnect to this initial dominion (kingly rule) potential.

You must apprehend what has ALREADY BEEN GIVEN. Beloved, this truth is for you.

---

1. See my book "Connecting," that addresses the idea of lost perception at the Fall. And the course, "The School of the Apostles" for understanding Apostolic Authority.

Mentions

Melchizedek is only mentioned twice in the Old Testament (Gen. 14:8, Ps. 110:4).

> Moses made two trips to the top of Mt. Sinai – each lasting 40 days and nights. Perhaps he learned about the people before him and the ages past on top of Mt. Sinai. Moses wrote the book of Genesis and about Abraham and Melchizedek over 425 years after they lived.

> King David wrote the Psalms, "The LORD (Yahweh-Eloheim) has sworn, and will not repent, Thou art a priest for ever after the order of Melchizedek" (Ps. 110:4). 1050 years later, Jesus was born.

The New Testament tells about Melchizedek in the book of Hebrews. Since this study is largely in Hebrews, we must understand more about it.

Hebrews was probably written before the fall of Jerusalem and the destruction of the temple in A.D. 70. Christians were wavering and in much despair and this letter is an appeal to them to persevere.

There's lots of conjecture as to who authored the Book of Hebrews. Many versions of the Bible place a heading over Hebrews stating, "The Epistle of Paul the Apostle to the Hebrews." However, that attribution was not part of the original document of Hebrews. The word patterns are not consistent with Paul's other letters.

Some think it was written by an associate of Paul's – maybe Timothy, Barnabas, Apolos, Silas, Aquilla, Luke – or perhaps Phoebe. In more recent times, some scholars have advanced a strong case for the authorship of Hebrews belonging to Priscilla.

We really don't know who wrote it. However, the Book of Hebrews was written to the Jews during massive persecution and many were returning to the Mosaic law.

Much to Say – Hard to Understand

As we mentioned in the introduction, the author tells us that about this subject of Melchizedek there is "MUCH TO SAY" and it is "HARD TO EXPLAIN" (Heb. 5:10-11).

Why is it hard to explain about Melchizedek? The author of Hebrews tries to address some critical basics, but their spiritual condition makes it "hard" for the reader to understand and hard for the author to explain.

Maybe this discussion about Aaron and Melchizedek sounded too academic and boring to the Hebrew readers. They were said to be "dull of hearing" and that's not just an ear problem, but a problem with the heart. Maybe they weren't really interested in what God had to say.

- Because you are slow to learn (vs.11).
- But they are still babies. In the original language, the sense of this is, "for they have become babies." There is nothing more irritating than someone who should be mature but who has later become a babe!
- Babies need a lot of sleep – (they are spiritually asleep).
- Babies fuss and cry over any little thing (immature).
- Babes are weak in discernment, and will accept any kind of spiritual food.
- They should be mature by now!
- By this time you ought to be teachers, but you need someone to teach you the elementary truths of God's word all over again (12).

MILK

The Hebrews author rebukes the readers for their unsatisfactory progress. "I have a lot to say to you, but your hearing is dull and sluggish. You need someone to teach you the fundamentals once again. If you only drink milk you are childish, unable to speak (unfit to bear weapons, *metalambano is* word play for someone not yet fifteen)." Paul told the Corinthians that because they were carnal (babes, natural people) he fed them with milk and not with solid food (1 Cor. 3:1-2).

- Babies need milk, not solid food (vs. 12) to grow.
- Milk drinkers are not acquainted with the teaching about RIGHTEOUSNESS (remember this one!).

Milk is a spiritual metaphor that refers to the basic doctrines and understandings of Christianity: salvation, resurrection of the dead, and the judgment, etc. Milk is what is necessary to begin to walk in salvation. We must always be aware of those who still need milk.

Either babies drink milk and experience spiritual growth and spiritual understanding or their growth is stunted.

Meat

Those that still live by milk alone are "unskillful in the word of righteousness." (v 13) Sure milk is necessary, but as believers become "skilled" concerning the Word of righteousness, it's time to eat MEAT.

THIS BOOK IS SOLID FOOD... Solid food is the "meatier" Truths such as understanding the connection between Jesus and Melchizedek. It is about being "skilled in RIGHTEOUSNESS!"

Melchizedek teaching is the "meat" of the gospel, which means for the mature (1 Cor. 3:1-3, 1 Pet. 2:2). Strong MEAT is for the believers who have exercised their senses to DISCERN (increase their capacity and potential) *good and evil* (from Heb. 5:14-15).

Meat gives discernment. Eating of Good and Evil embraces the Law of sin and death and must be discerned.

We can not obtain our Melchizedek priesthood through endless works and struggling to keep the Law.

MEAT takes our understanding beyond our initial concepts. This is called "maturity." Meat is for those growing up (Gal. 3:7). As we grow, our concepts about basic fundamental doctrines expand and develop.

Meat Digests Progressive Current Truth.

If you are not grown, then "strong meat" may cause you to get a stomachache and not able to digest your food.

Any meat you eat must first be cut into bite sized pieces in order for you to swallow it.

Your BODY chemically, physically, and biologically changes the structure and substance of "meat" as it moves past the intestines.

Meat transforms into a different state as it is digested - none of the original properties are the same.

Meat molecularly transforms into being a NEW part of YOU. It is called protein - a necessary building block for your lives.

What remains and is not transformed, must be eliminated.

Spiritual MEAT TRANSFORMS you and like natural meat, what is needed will be absorbed into the bloodstream.

"And the Lord said, "Who then is that faithful and wise steward, whom *his* lord shall make ruler over his household, to give *them their* portion of *MEAT* in due season? Blessed *is* that servant, whom his lord when he comes shall find him so doing. He will make him ruler over all that he has" (Lk. 12:42-44). Notice that the faithful and wise steward serves meat in the right season, even when no one is watching. Serving meat defines stewards as wise and faithful!

Jesus told the disciples in Samaria that He had MEAT that they did not know – and His *MEAT* was to DO the WILL of the Father (Jn. 4:32).

You EAT MEAT to discover and do God's will – that's spiritual nourishment.

Why Do We Want To Eat Meat?

MEAT is not an elitism about KNOWING more than someone else! We're not talking about gaining intellectualism or scholarship. It is NOT about political causes and not about the latest Bible fads. It is not about becoming proficient in Greek or Aramaic. IT IS about the ability to discern and deliver Truth that will protect the flock from false doctrines and 'ravenous wolves.'

Meat is heaven's bread. It's not oratory skills or brilliant scholarship. It's having deep hunger to "Come and Dine!" (Jn. 21:12). When dining, what do we hear? Three times Jesus tells Peter to "shepherd and FEED His lambs and sheep" (Jn. 21:15-17).

Hebrews tells us a remarkable Scripture differentiating the Old and New Covenant believers. No other New Testament book speaks about the details of this sacrifice discussed in Exodus "We have an altar, whereof they have NO RIGHT TO EAT which serve the tabernacle" (Heb. 13:10) This spiritual MEAT of the New Covenant reveals what Jesus has given us.

Meat is a type of the sacrificial body of Jesus who died as a ransom for us. God promises His new priesthood a "right to eat at a different altar" (Heb. 13:10). This heavenly altar contains the body and blood of Jesus – He alone qualifies us to eat the MEAT of this new day.

Hebrews goes on to say that we can only "go on unto perfection (maturity) IF GOD PERMITS" (Heb 6:1-3).

My friend, if there is any expectation for us to emerge as the triumphal Church, be assured that it will come from allowing the MEAT of God's Word about Melchizedek to transform us!

Lord, we entrust our lives to You and commit to study the meat of Your Word. We boldly come to You with the revelation that we have the right to eat MEAT.

So, if you are still with me, let's begin!

SECTION 1

Abram and Melchizedek

Bouts_Aelbert_Bentinck_Meeting_Abraham_Melchisedek Casa-in-italia image

Abraham

Abram's travels stretched over 1050 miles, from Ur (rhymes with *"poor"*) of the Chaldees in Mesopotamia, to near Jerusalem.

This ancient city of Ur was enclosed around by a high brick wall. The very small houses inside were made of mud bricks. Some say that Ur was the oldest most wonderful city in the whole world. Today this land is called Iraq.

The Chaldeans inhabitants spoke a language that was a precursor to what is now known as Hebrew. They invented the first war chariots – and that made them feared by other nations.

People of Ur prayed to dozens of wooden and stone carved idols that they believed had magical powers. Monotheism (or the worship of one god) was not present at this time.

> Epiphanius (died a.d. 403), Bishop of Salamis on the island of Cyprus, said that Terah (Abrams father) sculpted his own idols.
>
> An eighth-century Muslim text said, "Azar [Terah] used to make idols which his people worshipped."

Perhaps the idolatry was one reason why the Lord decided to take Abram away from Ur, "Get the out of your country, and from your kindred, and from your father's house, unto a land that I will show you" (Gen. 12:1). In other words, he said, "Come out of your past environment and to leave everything in the past."

ABRAHAM

Abram was a moon worshipper, but the Lord had a plan... notice the promise (Gen. 12:24):

• God said He would make Abram a great nation.

• I will bless you.

• I will make YOUR NAME GREAT.

• I will bless those who bless him and curse those who curse him.

God told Abram that his descendents would be numerous (Gen.13:16). But because of his advancing age, Abram asks God how this can be, when he continues to be childless (Gen.15:2-3). In Genesis 15:4, God tells Abram that a son would be born from his own body and that he would have a multitude of descendants" (Gen. 17:1-2).

A Name -- A SEED!

God promised Abram, "I will make your name great!" (Gen. 12:24)

The choice of names was always important. Within the name holds the destiny of that person. It determined how others saw that person – what his capacity and function would be.

Abram's name meant a "father of heights, a lofty father, a high father." Twenty four years after Abram and Lot began their sojourning, the Lord made even stronger covenant with Abram who was then ninety, and his name was changed to 'Abraham' (father of nations).

> Then, God again renews His covenant with Abram: "... No longer will your name be Abram. Instead, your name will be Abraham because I will make you the father of a multitude of NATIONS. I will make you extremely fruitful. NATIONS of you, and kings will descend from you (Gen. 17:4-6).

GOD'S NAME:

The name of God in the Old Testament, that occurs most frequently (6,823 times) is the so-called Tetragram, YHWH. Many Jews view this not as a name, but as epithet (a title of an aspect of God). YHWH is thought to be an ancient third person singular imperfect of the verb "to be" (meaning, "He is").

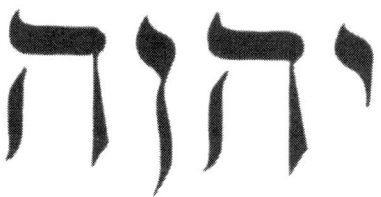

Whenever a Rabbi or any Jew read any written name of God, "YHWH", he orally replaced it with "Adonai," not "Yahweh." In those days, no one was allowed to speak the name YHWH out loud with their lips. His NAME was so sacred that it could not be uttered.

His name was the holy sound of breath. When God (*Yahweh*) made Abram's name "great," He added the same sound of His name (*Ha*) inside Abram and Sarai's name. The Lord God added the SOUND of His NAME (like the holy breath of creation) to theirs. This is covenant language – the expression of El Elyon, the God Most High who is Yahweh.

> Here, Abram (Noble Father) becomes AbraHAm (Father of many).

> Sarai (Princess) becomes SarAH (Mother of Nations).

> In conversation, Jewish people called God, HaShem, which is Hebrew for "the Name" (see Lev. 24:11). (Note the HA sound, and also see endnotes.)

> Abraham became the progenitor of a royal Kingdom nation.

> "To the one who is victorious, I will give some of the hidden manna. I will also give that person a white stone with a new name written on it, known only to the one who receives it (Rev. 2:17 NIV).

Hebrew

Abram was first called a "Hebrew" in Genesis 11:26, 14:13.[2] That word "Hebrew" probably refers to being a descendant of Eber (Gen. 11:16) who was an earlier descendant of Shem. (Eber is related to both Shem and Abram. And... Jesus, in His humanity, also descended from Abraham.)

> The likely origin of name "Eber" is derived from "br" which means "to cross over a boundary."

> The word for Hebrew also has to do with the "breath of God blowing."

Genealogies were of special significance to all of Israel. That way, others could identify Abram and the rest of his descendants as being Hebrews as well. This promise was made to Abraham and his SEED:

> The son Isaac was the promised natural SEED. "Isaac is the son through whom your descendants (your seed) will be counted" (Heb. 11:18).

> We are Abraham's SEED. The Divine Seed of the redeemed is us as the adopted spiritual children.

Two Kinds Of Seeds

There are two SEEDS – representing the spirit and the flesh. Abraham had natural children and he also became the father of all believers who received grace that produces a FAITH that produces RIGHTEOUSNESS (Rom. 5:12).

Again, on Mount Moriah, an angel promised Abraham that he would be blessed and that his children were to be numbered like the STARS in the sky and the SAND on the seashore (Gen. 22:15-17).

---

2. Principle of FIRST MENTION.

SAND SEEDS:

Sand is earthly and sand-seeds are the natural children of Abraham.

I will give you so many descendants that, like the dust of the earth, they can not be counted (Gen. 13:14-16). (12 Tribes)

I will multiply your descendants until they become as numerous as the sands on the seashore – too many to count (Gen. 32:12).

Every grain of sand in the world is unique when viewed through a microscope.

STAR SEEDS:

Every star is different when viewed through a telescope.

"Look at the sky and count the stars if you can. That's how many descendants you will have!" And Abram believed the Lord and the Lord counted him as righteous because of his faith" (Gen. 15:3-6).

"The *real* children of Abraham, are those who put their faith in God" (Gal. 2:6-7). Believers.

Now to Abraham and his SEED were the promises made. This is not a plural SEEDS, but "to your seed" who is Christ (Gal. 3:16).

"Where is the newborn king of the Jews? We saw his star as it arose, and we have come to worship Him" (Mat. 2:1-2).

STARS SET THE TIMES AND SEASONS[3]

"And God said, 'Let there be lights in the vault of the sky to separate the day from the night, and let them serve as signs to mark sacred seasons (times), and days and years'" (Gen. 1:14).

The lights of heaven determine the seasons and our calendar.

---

3. Carl Sagan famously said, "the total number of stars in the universe is greater than all the grains of sand on all the beaches on the planet Earth." It is estimated that the total number of 'all' grains of sand on earth are approximately 2000 billion billion. Scientists still think there are more stars in the Universe.

Prophetic seasons are established by the lights.

For those (people) who live in a land of deep darkness, a light will shine (Is. 9:1-2).

You are a city set on a hill (Matt. 5:14).

Abraham's blessing was given to both spiritual and natural Israel.

STAR-SEEDS	SAND-SEEDS
Descendents who are reborn of faith (Jn. 1:12-13, Gal. 3:6-7)	Natural Descendents from Abraham's
All the families on earth blessed (Gen. 12:1-3). A new race of people full of faith	Natural sons
Those who govern the Kingdom of God	Those who are subjects in the Kingdom
Spiritual Israel – Spiritual Children	Natural Israel – Natural Children
Men and women from every race and class	Israelites
True Israel of God (Gal. 6:16)	The Jewish Nation
Raised from the dead in this lifetime (Eph. 2:6)	Existing day to day
Seated with Christ in heavenly places (realms) (Eph. 2:6)	In this world
The Church - Israel of God, Holy Nations	The Nation of Israel

Soon, God entered into an ongoing covenant with Abram, promising prominence and possessions.

- I will bless you
- I will multiply your seed as the stars of heaven
- And as the sand on the seashore
- Your seed shall possess the gate of your enemy
- In YOUR SEED shall all the nations of the earth be blessed
- We are blessed because of faithful Abraham (Gal. 3:9)
- This blessing allowed the Gospel to come to the Gentiles (Gal. 3:14).

Melchizedek's blessing had already been purchased for Abram, because Jesus was "slain before the foundation of the world.

Remember this blessing was under the Old Covenant, but it was a shadow of what was to come.

SECTION 2

A KING

Melchizedek Was a King

We discover in Hebrews that Jesus gives us this Melchizedek priesthood. If this is our priesthood, how do we walk in it? What does it mean to you?

And that's why we ask, Who was Melchizedek and where did he come from?

Melchizedek is a name containing two words, the first is *"Melch"* which means "king." Melchizedek was a King.

- A king has authority to rule.
- A King has a Kingdom
- A King rules in dominion over his kingdom, a domain, a territory, or a jurisdiction.
- A king has subjects under him to whom he has the right and power to give orders.
- A king has authority and power to accomplish his purposes.

Melchizedek Was The King Of Righteousness

Greek as a language is abstract, but Hebrew's words are full of the nitty-gritty of daily life. They embrace ideas that can be applied here and now, to what life really means.[4]

Hebrew words are built upon stories or pictures that express every day common life. With Hebrew words (like Melchizedek), they are built on the here and now. They are the concrete expression of what they are really all about.

The first part of his name (*melch*) means "king." The second part (*zedek, tsedeq, tezeq, tezek*) means "righteousness." Look at that again. That isn't just a title! This King RULED OVER righteousness. *Tsedeq* was his domain.

Melchizedek's rule was of a specific KINGDOM of *tsedeq* (the second half of his name). *Melchizedek was king of righteousness. That means righteousness was the ruling force of his realm.*

 Therefore, we who hold the Melchizedek King-Priesthood should rule over the domain of RIGHTEOUSNESS as our territory or jurisdiction.

A king (man or woman) has jurisdiction — a command and influence over an area. The amount of territory you command as a kingdom assignment is called your *metron* or measure of rule.

---

4. Famous Orthodox Picture -- unknown origin

> His throne, crown and scepter represent the authority to rule that jurisdiction. (IE, The king of Spain rules over Spain. And every nation that Spain conquers became his subjects.)

Okay, so we rule over righteousness... but, what is righteousness? The meaning of this word has been lost to us.

The meaning of righteousness has baffled scholars for centuries. Many think it means "right standing before God." And, this understanding has caused believers to "try to become righteous." It caused us to build religious expectations of HOW we can BECOME *more* righteous. But, if we dig further, we see that there's much more than being in a "right standing with God."

Tzedek is the Melchizedek Rule

Over the years the word *righteous* has gotten a bad name, maybe because it has been confused with being self-righteous – full of ourselves, rather than full of God. But it doesn't mean that at all!

Most misunderstandings cling to one verse in the Bible that is taken out of context. Romans 3:10 says, "There is none righteous, no, not one." But, you need to understand that Paul is talking about Jews and Greeks who are evil and sinful. Notice that in Romans 3:19, Paul says these same people are under the law.[5]

---

5. Painting by Gavin Findly, MD, 2004

 Righteousness is for the believer. And, truth is – nobody is righteous by them self – but believers are righteous because *already* Jesus made them righteous.

In both the Old Testament and the New Testament, the word *righteousness* and *justice* have the same meaning. Only one Hebrew word (*tsedeq*) and one Greek word (*dikaios*) is used for both.

Tsedeq (tsedeq, tzedek, tsedek, zedeq) appears more than 250 times in the OT. Most of the time, *tsedeq* translates either RIGHTEOUSNESS or JUSTICE, or that which is already just.

Tsedeq comes from a Semitic word meaning to be a firm, straight, "like steel," determined integrity that goes to one's core. In Arabic, this means that one is "fully developed, balanced and mature."

Tsedeq (justice and righteousness) also incorporates RIGHT LIVING, equity, bounty, health, and prosperity.

Tsedeq means RIGHT RELATIONSHIPS AMONG ALL THINGS IN CREATED ORDER.

Tsedeq is the blessing of the God Most High to Abram (Gen. 14:22).

Prosperity

 *Tzedek* comes from a Semitic word meaning PROSPERITY. Think about that! Melchizedek was the KING OF PROSPERITY! Jesus, gives us His priesthood, which in turn allows us to rule a prosperous and balanced dominion. This is how we influence the world. This is our sign of strength – and how we can effectively move to occupy territories.

Tsedeq means the right relationships among all things in the created order of things... Tsedeq HOLDS THE "WORLD IN BALANCE." It is a right internal alignment with God's nature and His truth.

The clearest understanding 'tsedeq' means BALANCE and PROSPERITY – and that includes God's ways of Right living in health, equity, bounty, and true wholeness.

Jesus already gave it to us. Hebrew prosperity = "to push forward." to exceed, to bring success, to complete a mission, or to have increase and prosperity – in every area of life.

> This profoundly deep concept of prosperity does not come because of my ability, but it does come by understanding GOD'S imputed gift to me.

Tsedeq is the Godly force of energy that brings all things into the right internal alignment with God's nature and His Truth – the created order. In this way, Melchizedek includes a "total domination over prosperity (which includes wholeness, fullness, and finances), which in turn balances the world as a whole."

We can be and must become KINGS OF PROSPERITY. This king-priest role of Melchizedek blends both the spiritual and the temporal. It reaches eternally.

- *Tsedeq* as prosperity, balance, health, maturity, and right living is our domain and must rule over it.

As we RULE the earth in prosperity and balance, we mandate heaven's rule. God's KINGDOM is manifested on earth as we step into it.

Jesus is the King of Kings

In His humanity, Jesus is the KING. The genealogical lineage in the Book of Matthew claims His right to the Throne of David through his earthly father Joseph.

Pilate asked Jesus, "Are you the king of the Jews?" Jesus said, "Is that your own idea or did others talk to you about Me?"

"My KINGDOM is NOT OF THIS WORLD. If it were, My servants would fight to prevent My arrest...."

"You are a king, then!" Pilot replied.

Jesus answered, "YOU ARE RIGHT IN SAYING THAT I AM A KING. In fact, FOR THIS REASON I was born, and for this I came into the world... to testify to the TRUTH" (Jn. 18:33-38).

> His Kingdom speaks Truth. That is what makes His Kingdom different from all earthly kingdoms.
>
> He is the King of Kings and the everlasting ruler over the kings of the earth (Rev. 17:14).
>
> Jesus rules today as our King over the New Jeru-SALEM (Rev. 21:2, 24) that comes out from heaven.
>
> Jesus gives all of His citizens the right to be kings themselves.
>
> Jesus is the KING OF KINGS (Acts 17:7, 1 Tim. 1:17, 6;13, Rev 19:16).

Jesus embodied righteousness for us and gives us the ability to rule by faith in *tsedeq* (prosperity, maturity, and balance).

> Jesus waits in heaven until everything is restored to dominion (kingly rule).
>
> As His Kingdom rule progresses on earth, His rule IN US is visible.

Jesus is The Lord our Righteousness

Jesus, gives us His priesthood, which in turn allows us to rule a prosperous and balanced dominion (kingly rule). This is how we influence and impact the world. This is our sign of strength -- and how we can effectively move to occupy territories.

Righteousness and Justice are the attributes of God and His Kingdom.

> *Tsedeq is a redemptive NAME of the LORD!* Jesus IS THE Yahshua *Adonai Tzidkenu! The Lord our Righteousness.*

Jeremiah 23:6 "In his days Judah shall be saved, and Israel shall dwell safely: and this is his name whereby he shall be called, 'THE LORD OUR RIGHTEOUS'NESS.'" Jeremiah's prophecy told the name Adonai Tzidkenu (יְהֹוָה צִדְקֵנוּ), "THE LORD OUR RIGHTEOUSNESS." And the appearing of the "Righteous Branch" (*tzemach tzaddik*) (Jer. 23:5-6). This Righteous Branch is also mentioned in the Book of Zechariah.

> The *Midrash Lamentations* says, "A Proper name of Messiah is *Adonai Tzidkenu* - the Lord our RIGHTEOUSNESS."

> "Clouds and thick darkness surround him; righteousness and justice are the *foundation* of his throne" (Ps 97:2).

> Righteousness (*tsedeq*) and justice are the foundation of your throne; love and faithfulness go before you (Ps 89:14).

"I will betroth (pledge and guarantee of marriage) you to Me forever; Yes, I will betroth you to Me in RIGHTEOUSNESS (*tsedeq*) and in justice, in loving kindness (*hesed*) and in compassion (*rahamim*), and I will betroth you to Me in faithfulness (*emunah*). Then you will know the LORD" (Hos. 2:19-20).

> The gifts offered to secure this marriage are, righteousness, justice, loving kindness, compassion, and faithfulness – in other words, the Lord offers WHO HE is as a pledge of marriage.

> *Hesed* is the fundamental constituent of this covenant.

> *Emunah* is the reliable consistency of God to keep His promises.

 Righteousness means you DON"T have to "try to be good!" You are in Christ, who *already* became for you righteousness... (1 Cor. 1:30).

> 1 Corinthians 1:30 says, "And because from Him you have your life in Christ Jesus, Whom God made our Wisdom... manifesting itself as] our RIGHTEOUSNESS [thus making us upright and putting us in right standing with God], and our Consecration [making us pure and holy], and our Redemption [providing our ransom from eternal penalty for sin]." He is RIGHTEOUSNESS for us!

Kingdom

We who are of the Order of MELCHIZEDEK are to be KINGS of TZEDEK! Let's look at the Kingdom where we rule!

From the start, God's intention was to build His Kingdom on the earth by using His creation of humans to be co-creators with Him.

Jesus did not come to earth and die just to start a religion! There are many reasons why He came, but primarily:

> Jesus died to atone for the sins of the world (Heb. 2:17). But, this is not all!
>
> Jesus died so that we could obtain forgiveness!
>
> Jesus died to establish an unshakable Kingdom (Heb. 10:31)
>
> Jesus died to give us the authority to rule and to be like HIm.

We fully accept the imperative importance of the suffering and crucifixion of Christ. Now, we also look at what Jesus did in His ascension. He calls us farther. He gives us the Holy Spirit to lead us forward.

Matthew 6:33 says to seek FIRST the KINGDOM of God and His RIGHTEOUSNESS, and all these things shall be added to you. We seek it first, because that is what Jesus brought us!

When He rose from the dead, the Kingdom CAME! The Kingdom is here! Jesus died to bring forth the KINGDOM -- God's government on earth. Do we believe it? Can we apprehend what has already been given. Seek for it FIRST!

Jesus BUILDS His Church (Mat. 16:18) and He GIVES us the Kingdom (Mt. 16:18, 19).

The Prosperous FORCE of Melchizedek

In our recent past, many serious problems resulted from some extreme hyper-teaching on prosperity that misused the concepts MAINLY for self-indulgence. Unfortunately, excessive teachings on prosperity have left many confused and injured.

The Scriptures say over and over that what is in your heart (your belief system) is what develops in your life! HOW DO YOU SEE your situations? Because... that's what will happen.

Having a POVERTY MINDSET means that you don't FULLY SEE GOD FOR WHO HE IS AND WHO HE WANTS TO BE IN YOU... The job of the Holy Spirit is to reprogram the mind and help us "put on" the new man. The "old man" sees the way things SEEM - or the natural self. The New Man receives progressive truth.

We continue this subject because Jesus gives you the Melchizedek Priesthood and this is also your territory of rule - so you need to know about it. This is an ongoing understanding. It unfolds as we proceed. It's about gaining a full TRANSFORMATION into a full Melchizedek Priesthood.

In the Kingdom, there's no misery! Blessings of spiritual, physical, and material prosperity are part of your covenantal rights of DIVINE inheritance! It is the realm of your Melchizedek rule. Prosperity is your right ... not for control, not for greed, or grasping – but so that God's purposes will be promoted without hindrance.

The Melchizedek priesthood rules over *tzedek* (prosperity)! Do you see the possibility to OWN THE GROUND of your MELCHiZEDEK ASSIGNMENT?

1 John tells us the well known Scripture, "I pray above all that you PROSPER, even as your soul prospers." This author was John... the "one Jesus loved." This was said by favored friend who LAID his HEAD ON the Lord's chest at the communion supper... that above all his desire for us was to prosper.

> The SOURCE Bible translates this verse (1 JN. 2), "My dear friend, I claim that you have a prosperous path with regard to all things and are completely healthy with regard to all things, just as your life has a prosperous path."
>
> Importantly, we notice the words, "I claim" (strong emphatic present case construction.) I claim what is already yours. I claim that you are already in this present time prosperous!
>
> Beloved, we CLAIM what is ours, we don't beg, we don't finagle! We apprehend it! This isn't hyper-faithism, this is Scripture. The Greek says that we are to claim things as if we already have them... they are ours now (right now in the present) if we believe.
>
> This verse talks about a prosperity that the early church reader understood to encompass the removal of difficulties, physical health, and material prosperity.
>
> (3), "... I have no greater joy than to hear that my children walk in the TRUTH."

IT'S A TRUTH THAT YOU CAN PROSPER. "God plans to prosper me and not harm me, to give me hope and a future" (Jer. 29:11).

Prosperity is the FORCE God gives you to fulfil His will in your life.

Apostolic minded Kingdom prayers enforce the idea of governing and ruling over the territories of the Kingdom that are given to us.[6]

The Melchizedek king/Priest transforms this world and the world systems. It is the eternal agency that has the custodial authority to advance the King-

---

6. For exact ideas on how to pray in this New Order, see my article, "Breakthrough Prayer" on http://kluane.com

dom until the kingdoms of this world have become the Kingdoms of our Lord and of His Christ (Rev. 11:15).

As our Melchizedek reign is fully expressed with us, we increase our influence.

The New Order of Melchizedek brings the intangible spiritual dimension to the tangible earth.

The Melchizedek process throughout our lives is to transform the Kingdom. The KINGDOM of God is a government that rules over the entire earth (Daniel 2:44).

Our personal interaction with this plan can alter the governmental nature of the UNIVERSE.

The Order of Melchizedek rules over Kingdom citizens and over all that is done in the Kingdom of God.

Summary:

 The OT word *tsedeq* & NT word for righteousness *diakinos*, have the SAME MEANING.

RIGHTOUESNESS is an imperative! The restoration of right relationship between humans and God. You can only be righteous by faith.

 OUR MELCHIZEDEK ASSIGNMENT IS TO MAINTAIN BALANCE AND RIGHT RELATIONSHIP OF PROSPERITY AMONG ALL THINGS IN THE CREATED ORDER.

> **TSEDEQ = RIGHTEOUSNESS**
>
> RIGHT LIVING, BEING MORALLY RIGHT,
>
> **RIGHTWISENESS,**
> EQUITY, HEALTH, bounty, true prosperity,
> BALANCE
> PROSPERITY
> right relationships among all things in the created order of things.
>
> to be straight, firm, steel-like, as opposed to evil,
>
> Arabic equivalent = MATURE

Tsedeq, with all it embodies, includes prosperity, balance, health, maturity and right living. And this becomes our domain over which we rule.

Your Melchizedek priesthood gives you the POWER and authority TO CREATE IN YOUR WORLD, to determine the future, and to bless others with His favor.

The magnitude of this revelation is ongoing and ever unveiling. TZEDEK is your DOMINION RULE. IT is your apostolic governing platform.

> TZEDEK is the provision to enable your INFLUENCE.
>
> TZEDEK determines the reach of influence.

Position yourself to believe that you are already righteous because of Him! You are already fully acceptable in the beloved (Eph. 1:6). It's only through faith that you can grasp the Truth – that God is already in your midst. He's here. Your citizenship is *already* in heaven (Phil. 3:20).

It's about grasping the MEAT of the Spirit that will change the lives of those who will change the world. God looks for those mature believers to come forth who are congruent – whole in their mind and fully ready.

Dear Reader, I bless you today with the Melchizedek BLESSING of VICTORY and PROSPERITY. That you find even greater increase – past limiting understandings give way for the discovery of ongoing present TRUTHS (truths that are discovered jewels in our drawer of inheritance)... I claim that the inheritances of truth be revealed and discovered.

I declare that right now you do prosper and that you are in health even as your SOUL (mind, will, emotions) and life prosper... even now as the comprehension of your MINDSET expands, may you prosper!

The Battle

Abram was told in Genesis 12:10-13 to do three things:
- Get out of his country.
- Leave your family.
- Leave your father's house.
- Leave everything that keeps you in limitations. Leave the idolatry and the family traditions.

But, you know the story! Abram did not do what was commanded. He left taking his dad and his nephew Lot along with him (Gen. 12:4) – and they caused a lot of problems!

> Lot's name meant "veil." He carried a veil into the land – and we see this same blinding veil over many believers today. The veil restricts comprehension of all that was accomplished for us by the finished work of Jesus Christ.

Abram left Haran in 2085 BC and he built an altar at Shechem. He later moves to Egypt because of great famine.

To maintain his own safety, Abram forced Sarai to tell the King (Pharaoh) of Egypt and she was his sister! Historians point out that Sarah was indeed both

Abram's wife and sister, but because she was a half-sister by a different mother – and this was not considered an incest taboo.

Because Sarai was extraordinarily beautiful, the Pharaoh paid a bountiful treasure for her and took her to himself. He showered Abram with livestock and servants in order to gain her hand in marriage. Sarai became part of "Pharaoh's house" which is believed to mean part of his harem.

> The Rabbis tell that Hagar (Gen. 16:1) was an Egyptian princess and daughter of the Pharaoh of Egypt whom he gave to Sarah as a wedding gift along with gold, silver, slaves and lands (Pirkei de-Rabbi Eliezer [ed. Higger], chap. 26).
>
> This idea of Hagar being an Egyptian princess also appears in a Jewish records from the first century BCE (Genesis Apocryphon [ed. Avigad-Yadin], p. 37)
>
> The Midrash tells that the Pharaoh gives her his daughter Hagar as a handmaiden saying, "It would be better for my daughter to be a handmaiden in this house [i.e., Sarah's] than a noblewoman in another [in the palace in Egypt]."
>
> The Rabbis explain that when Pharaoh gave his daughter to Sarah he said, "This is your reward [agrekh]" (Midrash and Gen. Rabbah 45:1). Her name HaAgar means reward.
>
> Hagar is said to have grown up in the home of Abraham and Sarah, and later became the mother of Ishmael.

Obviously, Abram didn't have much of a moral fortitude at this time. God sends a plague to punish the adultery of Pharaoh. Pharaoh realizes the truth of the matter, and returns Sarai to Abram.

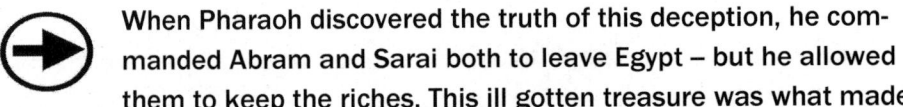

When Pharaoh discovered the truth of this deception, he commanded Abram and Sarai both to leave Egypt – but he allowed them to keep the riches. This ill gotten treasure was what made Abram "VERY RICH" (Gen 13:2). And this additional bounty caused arguments with his closest family. Abram prospered because of a lie that risked his wife's safety.

After the famine, they return to Canaan. Both Abram and Lot are now extremely wealthy. When Abraham and Lot negotiated over the ground to live on, it was because their illegal wealth was built on a lie. They had so much bounty that they didn't know how to manage it, and had to separate.

Dividing

Genesis 13 tells us how Abram returned to Canaan after the famine had passed and the lands became fertile again. By this time, his and Lot's sizeable livestock and both families occupying the same pastures became problematic (v.6,7).

There was strife between their herdsmen (Gen. 13:6-7). Conflicts ensued between herdsmen until Abram decided they should part ways, lest there be conflict amongst "brethren" (v.8,9) and "their possessions were too great for them to live together" (Gen. 12:6, AMP).

"Abram gave Lot first choice of where to live. He said, 'Is not the whole land before you?... If you take the left hand, then I will go to the right; or if you choose the right hand, then I will go to the left'" (12:9-11).

Lot looked beyond Jordan and saw a well watered plain, and chose that land, for it was like "the garden of the LORD" (before the destruction of Sodom and Gomorrah and the formation of the salt sea, Gen. 13:9-11). Lot chose the eastern Jordan valley and moved his tents in view of Sodom.

Abram headed south to Hebron, staying within the land of Canaan. He dwelt by the terebinth trees of Mamre where he built an altar to worship the Lord (Gen. 13:12,18). Abraham allowed the Lord to choose the best location for himself.

Sodom was a place of tropical luxuriance. But, it is a *type* of the wickedness of this world. Lot pitched his tent toward Sodom (where he could still see the town) and later moved his tents down the Jordan valley (adjacent to the Dead Sea) until he came near to Sodom (Gen 13:12). Eventually his heart was vexed and he actually lived in that wicked city of Sodom (13:13, 14:12). (The sin of this world can ensnare your righteousness.)

Sin is "flagrant" there (Gen. 18:20-21, 19:4-8).

Lot went to Sodom as a wealthy farmer.

In Genesis 19:1, Lot is seen sitting in the gateway of Sodom, a place reserved for the business leaders of the community. (The commerce of this world.)

Although Lot was known to be "RIGHTEOUS" and not like the people of Sodom, he was "caught up unaware" by his association with them. Because he pitched his tent near evil, his heart was ensnared (Prov. 1:10-16).

When Lot dwelled with Abram, he could partake of the blessing. But, when Lot was not living with Abram, he suffered loss.

Lot lost everything he had – not just once, but twice! Abraham was the one who saved him both times (Gen 14 & 19).

Good Decision

God was please how Abram handled this situation with Lot. He reminds Abram of His promises and even adds to them. In Chapter 12, the promise was only that land would be given to Abram's descendants. But now (Chap. 13), when Abram was in Hebron, vs. 18) he was told to "lift up his eyes" and look around... then, the Lord adds three more elements.

Abram will have countless descendants.

He and his descendants would be given all the land Abram could see or set his foot upon.

They would possess the land forever.

That is still a promise to us, the children of Abraham. As far as we can perceive will be given. Inheritance is a matter of perception! (You will see that *perception* is a theme running throughout this book.)

The War

"Now the men of Sodom were *wicked* and were sinning greatly... (13:13). The word, "wicked" is the Hebrew verb *rhea'* meaning to "be bad, evil." It is often used as the antonym of good, as in "good and evil."

As this story continues, a war ensued. This was the first major World War in the history of mankind – the slime-pit War of the Four Kings against the Five Kings. This war was fought during the days of Amraphel (who according to several Jewish scholars was also known as Hammurabi, and perhaps the same person as Nimrod).

At that time, Amraphel was, king of Shinar, Arioch was king of Ellasar, Chedorlaomer was king of Elam, and Tidal ruled as king of Goyim. They waged war against Bera, king of Sodom, Birsha, king of Gomorrah, Shinav, king of Admah, Shemever, king of Tzevoyim, and the king of Bela, now Tzoar - all of them wicked as well.

The four kings, led by Chedorlaomer defeated the five kings that was led by Bera (the name of the wicked king of Sodom). Bera LOST!

 These names are detailed here because these Kings represent the HUMAN NATURE over which Abram needed Victory! The names of these kings represent the forces that we must conquer.

1. The four invader Kings of the valley were:

    Amraphel KING OF BABYLONIA. His name means WORLDLINESS. He was from the South (Gen. 10:8-9).[7] (Hammurabi.)

Arioch King of Shinar (CONFUSION). Shinar is believe to now be Syria, the northern part of that world.[8]

Chedorlaomer King of Elam (HIDDEN DISTANT). This King was the leader of the coalition, seeking to enlarge his empire, which was Persia.

Tidal (FEARFUL) King of nations (a united group of smaller nations).

2. **The five defending Kings:**

Bera King of <u>Sodom</u> (SCORCH AND BURNING), located in the Vale of Siddim.

King Birsha (WICKEDNESS) King of Gomorrah (in the Vale of Siddim).

Shinab (TURNING INDECISION) King of Admah (OLD NATURE).

Shemeber (CONSPICUIOUS INDIVIDUALITY) King of Zeboiim.

King Bela (DEVOURING DESTRUCTION and CONFLICT) of Zoar (LITTLE).

7. The Torah says that Amraphel is Nimrod.
8. The Genesis Apocryphon (from the Dead Sea Scrolls) identifies Ellasar (Shinar) with *kptwk* evidently "Cappadocia" which is exactly where Pontus lies just south of the Black Sea.

The War

King Cheldorlaomer ruled the five king-nations of the valley. This valley was a strategic location between Egypt and Mesopotamia and it was the pivotal place that controlled travel and communication going through the area.[9]

Five king-city-states at the south end of the Dead Sea paid tribute to Cheldorlaomer for twelve years. In year 13 year, they rebelled and stopped paying tribute. The four Mesopotamian kings brought in their armies to punish the five rebellious city-states. These five nations in the valley rebelled and in the thirteenth year an intense battle ensued.

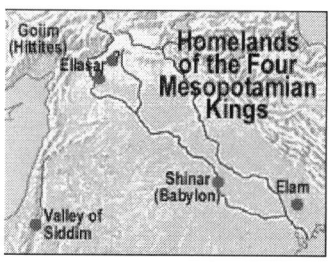

The 5 King coalition forces marched down the Jordan Valley until they reached the Vale of Siddim (later called the Valley of the Salt Sea or Dead Sea), and marched east fighting this ongoing war mainly in slime pits (Gen. 14:3, 8, 10). [10]

The valley of Siddim at the south end of the Salt sea, are now probably under water.[11]

Eventually, the four Mesopotamian kings won this massive war. They plundered Sodom and took all the Sodom residents captive – along with Abram's nephew Lot and all his possessions.

This huge entourage moved forward with the four victorious kings,

---

9. Photo, "In Swift Vengeance," Abraham in a surprise attack on the Mesopotamian kings, by American Illustrator Tom Lovell (1909-1997)

10. The word "tar pits" or "slime pits" is the Hebrew noun hēmār, "bitumen, asphalt." The material was abundant in the Dead Sea area, was used as mortar and sealant (Gerard Van Groningen, TWOT #683b). The description of the smell of Sodom may have been the combustion of petroleum gases from the bituminous deposits in the area. This could have caused seismic disturbances, which caused the area to sink some 20 feet under the surface of the Dead Sea. In 1953, significant petroleum deposits were discovered in the region.

11. Map, http://www.jesuswalk.com/abraham.htm

The Convergence

Abraham lived in the plains of Mamre at nearby Hebron when God began to negotiate with Abraham about the extreme wickedness of Sodom and Gomorrah, "Shall I hide from Abraham what I am doing"? (Gen. 18:17).

> We are not sure with whom the Lord was having this discussion! After all, the cities in the plain now belonged to Abraham as his promised land.
>
> The Lord wanted Abraham to know about the coming destruction of Sodom before it happened.
>
> Abraham had the authority to try to negotiate with God about Sodom.
>
> Abraham could have simply asked that Lot be safe… but instead he cried out for all the righteous living there to be spared.

Remember that the Lord instigated Abraham's prayer by telling him what was about to happen. "Abraham stood yet before the LORD" (Gen.18:1-22) and boldly pleaded on behalf of the people of Sodom, where Lot dwelt (again).

Abraham appealed to the Lord's justice. "Would You also destroy the RIGHTEOUS (*zaddikim*) with the wicked?" (vs. 23)

> Here we find one of the greatest prayers of the Bible. Abraham's interactive plea for Sodom and Gomorrah allows us hear the conversation.

Abraham asked the Lord to spare the city if as few as fifty righteous (tzedeq) could be found. Yes, the Lord agreed, "If I find in Sodom fifty RIGHTEOUS within the city, then I will spare the whole place on their account." (Verse 26)

You probably know the story. Abraham did not stop… What about 45? 40? 30? 20? And finally - 10. The Lord agreed, "I will not destroy it on account of the ten" (vs. 32).

> This prayer shows the insistence of Abraham and the mercy of the Lord. We can learn from this negotiation. Abraham knew the nature of the Lord

Tsedeq embodies God's rule (Ps 96:11). Think about this for a minute. The LORD told Abraham, "IF YOU FIND ME TEN RIGHTEOUS PEOPLE (*tsedeq*), I will rescue Sodom." However, there were not even ten people who lived their lives as fully mature and balanced. There weren't ten in the whole city who truly understood that prosperity and wholeness could be theirs.

The question is, are there ten mature and balanced in prosperity there in your town? Can the LORD find ONE who is TZEDEK?

> Now, look around and ask... Are there ten righteous (*tzedek*) right now?
>
> Are there *ten* who walk as mature and balanced believers who hold the world in balance?
>
> God Manages Things With Tsedeq (Ps 96:11).
>
> Notice also in Matthew 24:37-41 that the wicked are taken and only the RIGHTEOUS remain. The RIGHTEOUS are LEFT BEHIND! That fact should change some end time theories.

The Rescue

One man who had escaped from Sodom came to tell Abraham about this news of the war and about Lot being taken. When Abraham heard about the capture of his nephew, his actions set off world changing events.

Abraham immediately developed a plan to capture Lot! We must remember that he had never been a warrior – and he was not the King of any nation. Yet, he took decisive military action, that was not to gain land or possessions – but to rescue family.

(This is the same Abraham who earlier was willing to leave his wife with the Pharaoh of Egypt in order to escape and save his life, see 12:10-20).

He convinced Mamre, Eshcol, and Aner, his Amorite neighbors near Hebron, to join him. He made an alliance with these three "allies" (NIV) or "confederates" (KJV). This "alliance" is the Hebrew noun *berit*, meaning "covenant, treaty, agreement."

These Amorites would later become the enemies of the people of God.

Abraham gathered his 318 servants and together, they courageously pursued the enemy forces of the four wicked Kings to the northern part of Israel which was called Dan.

There, he strategically divided his men and attacked the enemy at night. The surprised army fled and Abraham continued the pursuit for over 120 miles till they past Damascus.

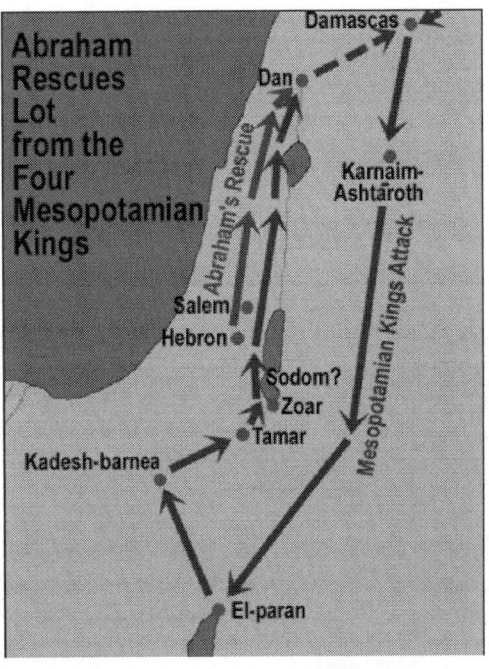

You can imagine how these four Armies were celebrating their win this night and enjoying their victory. They were surprised by this night attack.[12]

Amazingly, Abraham and his small band of fighters won their battle, rescued Lot, and took away the grand spoils of victory.

Abraham did not suffer any losses.

Abraham rescued Lot and the other inhabitants of Sodom and Gomorrah.

With Lot at his side, Abraham journeyed away from that battle.

That's when Abraham met Melchizedek who was the only king in this story who was not involved in conflict…

---

12. Drawing from http://www.jesuswalk.com/abraham.htm

SECTION 3

Priesthood of Melchizedek

Melchizedek Was a Priest

As Abraham proceeded back home with Lot, they encountered the King and Priest named Melchizedek. This Priest met Abram after he had won the war with the kings, and instructed him about this Great God.

 Melchizedek was the very FIRST PRIEST mentioned in the Bible. He was the "PRIEST OF THE MOST HIGH GOD" (El Elyon). Melchizedek was a king and also priest who performed priestly functions before the Levitical system was ever established.

His parentage is not known - which means this priesthood is not tribal. This is unusual, because the Levitical priesthood (that came later) was based on lineage. But, Melchizedek was not a Levite.

El Elyon

In this era of paganism and idolatry, Melchizedek worshiped El Elyon, the "God Most High." Melchizedek blessed Abram in the name of El Elyon (Gen. 14:18). This is the FIRST MENTION of El Elyon.

Before Abram left Ur, The Lord God presented Himself to Abram. In other words, Abram already understood God as Jehovah LORD (הוהי)

Melchizedek presented God primarily as *El Elyon* (אֵל עֶלְיוֹן), the supreme God Most High.

El Elyon – (Strongs 927) meaning "elevated, lofty, supreme, Most High, highest." Used 34 times in the Old Testament.

Elyon seems to be God the Father of our Lord Jesus Christ (Eph. 1:3). 37 times, Jesus is called the "Son of the Most High" (Mk. 5:7, Lk. 8:28).

THE OTHER "EL" NAMES OF GOD

- Eloheim (Gen. 1:1)
- El Shaddai 17:1
- El-beth-el (31:13)

Communion

This sculpture is Melchizedek (holding the cup), Chartres Cathedral, France

Melchizedek blessed Abram and brought forth bread and wine (Gen. 14:18).

It seems that Melchizedek brought the elements with him. This PRIESTLY action of serving of Bread and Wine distinguishes God El Elyon from other gods of that particular time.

 When Abram partook of the bread and wine, the Lord Most High God began revealing Himself in even a greater way.

This is an ongoing IMPERATIVE PRINCIPLE: the more God reveals Himself, the more we can see (comprehend, perceive) what He has given us.

Abram began to receive the progressive revelation about the promises that God had given him.

Victory of Communion

The giving of bread and wine was a PRIESTHOOD action of Melchizedek.

Abram partook of the emblems of the eternal priesthood that was to be revealed centuries later

Many events in the Old Testament foreshadow events in the New Testament, often without the participants realizing the importance of what they are going through. Surely, Abram did not know what that bread and wine would come to symbolize. This is typology of a priest mediating a Passover service and of course, a prefiguring reference to the Son who gave communion at the Upper Room (Mt. 26:26-28)

This is the FIRST MENTION of the symbols used in Communion.

During this exchange, the blessing flows out of a two way covenant. The Priest and King ministers from the Order of Melchizedek to the partaker.

This first foreshadowing of Communion was given to acknowledge and commemorate the great victory that had been won over the wicked kings.[13]

Bread and wine was the signature to begin the next part of his journey.

Just as Melchizedek brought out bread and wine to commemorate that victory, so Jesus brought out bread and wine at the Last Supper to commemorate His victory.

With Abram and with us, COMMUNION WAS/IS ABOUT VICTORY. We have VICTORY is WHAT WAS ACCOMLIPSHED AT THE CROSS! Jesus IS our victorious Priest forever (Ps. 2:7, Ps. 110:4).

"Therefore He had to be made like His brethren in all things, that He might become a merciful and faithful high priest in things pertaining to God, to make propitiation for the sins of the people" (Heb. 2:17).

Jesus is the bread that came from heaven, and the life is in the blood, "except you eat of the flesh of the Son of Man and drink His blood, you have no life in you" (Jn. 6:53 NKJ).

We are the PARTAKER of "flesh and blood" (Heb. 2:14-16, 10:5-7).

1 Corinthians tells us that the BREAD is His body and the CUP (wine) is His BLOOD. HIS BODY and BLOOD were the sacrifices at the cross (bread and wine). We must discern the body! (1 Cor. 11:29). Communion is reckoned as eating His flesh and drinking His blood, believing that His body bore our sins, and His sufferings brought us life.

This is the celebration before Jesus died. His death instituted the coming New Order. The KIngdom CAME! He told the disciples how to abide in Him and have eternal life; "Whoever eats (chews, gnaws) my flesh (meat) and drinks my blood has eternal life, and I will raise him up at the last day. For my

---

13. Painting by Dieric Bouts - The Meeting of Abraham and Melchizedek -- 1425-1485

flesh is REAL FOOD and my blood is real drink. The one who FEEDS (chews, gnaws) on me will live because of me. (Jn. 6:48-59).

The disciples said, "This teaching is too hard!" Jesus answered, "These words I have spoken to you are spirit and they are life." As a result of this statement, many disciples left!

After His death, at His Ascension, Jesus presented HIs atoning blood directly to the Father. It was not taken to the Mercy Seat in the natural physical temple in Jerusalem, but Jesus presented His PRIESTLY MELCHIZEDEK heavenly emblems of communion (His actual body and blood) to the Father. Then, Jesus sat down on the right hand of God as THE Melchizedek.

- The sacrifice could not be taken to the earthly temple because that earthly temple belonged to the Levitical Order.
- His sacrifice was for all humanity, not just the Jews.
- His Priesthood is superior to the old, and He mediates a better covenant based on better promises (Heb. 8:6).
- His priesthood operates in the everlasting ORDER of the Kingdom of heaven.

 Being a Melchizedek priest today means that He abides IN US – and we embody and become the bread and wine for all to partake. We offer ourselves.

The BLESSING

"And Melchizedek king of Salem brought forth bread and wine: and he was the priest of the most high God. And he blessed him, and said, 'BLESSED BE

Abraham OF THE MOST HIGH GOD, POSSESSOR OF HEAVEN AND EARTH'" (Gen. 14:18-19).

This blessing was a PRIESTHOOD action of Melchizedek.

This BLESSING WAS MADE BY THE WORDS SPOKEN. During this blessing, Abraham was set apart by the Lord.

W.E. Vine and Webster's Dictionary say that the word "bless" means "to cause to PROSPER, to make happy, to bestow favor upon, to consecrate to holy purposes, to make successful." Vines goes on to explain this definition, "TO MAKE PROSPEROUS IN TEMPORAL CONCERNS PERTAINING TO THIS LIFE, to guard and preserve."

The priestly act of blessing with WORDS is the TRANSFER OF FAVOR OR PRIVILEGE. These BLESSING words were spoken and SEALED with the bread and the wine brought to Abraham by Melchizedek.

Abraham was set apart and confirmed by this divine blessing.

God entered into a divine covenant with Abraham, promising land, prominence, and possessions. As Abraham's seed, this mandate STILL STANDS for us today.

These words were the words given by Melchizedek as a person authorized to declare God's intention and to bestow a phenomenal blessing upon Abraham.

These phenomenal and covenantal words of spoken blessing set off an ongoing process that still affect believers who are the Spiritual children of Abraham. This priestly act of blessing IS the transfer of favor or privilege.

The BLESSING

Abraham's blessing is YOUR inheritance! The Melchizedek Blessing upon Abraham enables you to be blessed and prosper no matter what circumstances may be. Faith is the key!

You not only receive the blessing, but because of Jesus, you become a Melchizedek PRIEST! NOW – YOU become the BLESSOR!

Not only does this blessing covenant belong to us, but the power of the Melchizedek priesthood in us, gives us the power to bless others.

Our JOB as Melchizedek priests is to BLESS!

As you pursue this giving of the Melchizedek blessing, it overtakes you. The power of blessing strengthens your life and this power can escalate even as you read this book!

The action of a Melchizedek priest is to bless (*barak*).

You can enter into this act of blessing: It is the transfer of favor or privilege.

Whatever we (as Melchizedek priests) bless and declare on earth, legally brings the *heavenly to earth*.

Jesus blessed His followers, and then was carried up into heaven on His own power (Lk. 24:51).

Look at Prov. 3:33, "The Lord blesses the home of the righteousness (zedek)! This place becomes A HABITATION where God can fill every corner with His presence.

This blessing reveals to Abraham the way that El Elyon looks at him.

Possessor of Heaven and Earth

"And he blessed him and said, 'Blessed be Abraham of the most high God, POSSESSOR OF THE HEAVENS AND OF THE EARTH; and blessed be the most high God, who has delivered thine enemies into thy hand'" (Gen. 14:19-20).

According to the literal Greek, that blessing was that Abraham would be a possessor of heaven and earth (Gen. 14:9). Later, Abraham generationally passed that blessing down to Isaac (Gen. 22:17), etc.

 Melchizedek's blessing can be translated that Abraham was given the gift of the world!

This blessing (to possess both *heaven and earth*) is here for every believer!

The substantiation for this idea that Abraham would be possessor of heaven and earth is that Romans tells us he was HEIR OF THE WORLD.

"It was not through the law that Abraham and his offspring received the promise that he would be HEIR OF THE WORLD Through the RIGHTEOUSNESS that comes by FAITH" (Rom. 4:13).

Remember, you are the seed of Abraham – his heir and the heir of the promise of Jesus. Of course, this promise is for you and you apprehend it by faith!

FAITH: Abraham is a hero of Faith because he received the promises by faith! In order to obtain the Melchizedek blessing, we must receive it by faith (just as Abraham did (Heb. 11:8).

"Even as Abraham believed God, and it was accounted to him for righteousness, know ye (present imperative) therefore that they which are of (*ek*) FAITH, the same are the children (sons) of Abraham... 'In thee shall all nations be blessed'" (Gal. 3:6-8).

***

Following the blessing and communion, Abraham tithed! To keep this story more understandable, we'll talk about it in a later chapter.

The Decision

When Abraham plundered the enemy's camp, he also confiscated all the gold and wealth that the Kings had looted from Sodom. As he led Lot away, he met with Melchizedek. Abraham partook of the bread and wine, received the blessing, and tithed to Melchizedek.

My favorite part of this story is here at this next part – the point of decision.

Here at the same time that Abraham was standing there with Melchizedek, when the King of Sodom suddenly appeared – right after the TITHE! (For any preachers out there, this will preach!)

The wicked King of Sodom had just lost the war. Yet, he still tries to intimidate and to confiscate what had been taken from him.

It seems no coincidence that the LORD revealed Himself to Abraham and they had the covenantal exchange of blessing and tithing right before the convergence with Sodom. Abraham had partaken of the heavenly Order and plan for his life, he had been changed. The blessing of Melchizedek gave him the ability to raise up against evil thinking and the gaining of dishonest fortune.

And because of what happens next, it seems probable that the tithe had sanctified his previous ill gotten gains from the Pharaoh (getting money for Sarai). We see that somehow, the power of this encounter with the Order of

Melchizedek gave Abraham the ability to discern right from wrong. While Abraham previously had difficulty, Abraham was now able to make right decisions. He was empowered!

Then, the king of Sodom comes out to meet him at the Valley of Shaveh (King's Valley) (Gen. 14:17).

> Valley of Shaveh (King's Valley): Shaveh <H7740> "plain" "peace"; also considered to be (Jerusalem)/

"And the king of Sodom, said unto Abraham, 'GIVE ME THE PERSONS, AND TAKE THE GOODS TO THYSELF.'"

 This doesn't make much sense at first glance... but actually, the Sodom king saw Abraham tithe to Melchizedek and he said, "I don't want your money or your tithe, I just want your (soul) goods!"

HERE at the intersection of blessing were two KINGS – Melchizedk and Sodom... Good and evil, Righteousness and Scorching. Giver and Taker. Life and Death. God or the world.

> There is another view of this Scripture (when Sodom said he didn't want the money), that he wanted the *people* who were taken captive by Abraham.
>
> But, the correct translation is that the King of Sodom did not want money (the TITHE), he wanted Abraham's SOUL. (The word translated as people is *nephesh* which the word for breath and soul.) This included his personality and the essence of who he was.
>
> "You keep the goods" (*rekuwsh*, property, goods, possessions, livestock,) etc.
>
> In other words, "You don't have to tithe to me... I don't want your money! I don't need money."
>
> According to King Bera of Sodom, Abraham could keep the wealth. (We know that Abraham was already VERY rich! He really didn't need more money.) With all the people of Sodom as Abraham's captives and the loot of all the nations, he could have started his own Kingdom...

"I want your SOUL! I want your allegiance and your covenant to be with me. You thoughts, your desires, and your person to be mine!"

But, Abraham said "NO!" He refused, saying to the King of Sodom: "… I have lifted up mine hand unto the Lord, the most high God (El Elyon), the possessor of heaven and earth, that I will not take from a thread even to a shoelatchet, and that I will not take any thing that is thine, lest thou would say, I have made Abraham rich" (Gen. 14:21-23).

- When Abraham turned from the King of Sodom, he renounced the world and committed his life to God.

- He VERIFIED THIS covenant with AN OATH, by raising his hand unto the LORD.

- Abraham had received two understandings about the LORD (*Jehovah*) and the extension of the revelation of Who the God was as El Elyon.

 The temptation is *always* FOR YOUR *SOUL*. Abraham maintained the integrity of his SOUL was by not keeping anything that came from Sodom!

Abraham learned about ill gotten gains from Egypt! He realized from past experience that he didn't want this money either. He knew there must be a better way to find Kingdom wealth.

So instead of taking Sodom's possessions, Abraham returns them – not keeping a shoestring. It seems that he returned everything – only allowing his soldiers keep what that had earned.

TWO KINGS MEET Abraham – AND THEY ARE OPPOSITES.

MELCHIZEDEK, KING OF SALEM	BERA, KING OF SODOM
Melchizedek = "King of Righteousness"	Bera = "be evil" (14:2)
Abraham ACCEPTS Melchizedek's blessings & bread and wine.	Abraham REJECTS Bera's offer
Salem = "Peace"	Sodom = Scorching and Burning
Priest of the Most High God	Worshipper of false Gods
Received Tithes	Refused Tithing - wanted SOUL

Abraham chose to live by FAITH and wait for another time for God's promise.

Abraham wouldn't have anything to do with the king of Sodom's suggestion because he was beginning to realize who God was and what the Divine plan was for his life was.

Abraham raised his hand to God, finally understanding that God's promises were not something to earn or gain by force – but that God would accomplish it Himself. Abraham represents all who are to receive salvation and the promise of righteousness... these are called spiritual Israel.

The Melchizedek blessing gives a discernment against worldly evil.

- Melchizedek gives King/priests the power to resist immortality (Sodom) and to rise up against perversion.
- Melchizedek gives King/priests the ability to not be involved with unlawful money (mammon).

SECTION 4

How the Priesthood Changed

The Priesthood Changed

Many modern churches still don't understand that we don't exist under the old Levitical order of things anymore! Let's expand this idea of WHY we need to fully change into this NEW ORDER:

Old Testament Priesthood

Over 400 years after Abraham tithed to Melchizedek, Moses received the Law and the Levitical Priesthood began. Let's take a quick look at how that happened.

Ex 19:3-6 Then Moses went up to God, and the LORD called to him from the mountain and said, "...Now IF YOU OBEY me fully and keep my covenant, then out of all nations you will be my treasured possession. Although the whole earth is mine, you will be for me a KINGDOM OF PRIESTS AND A HOLY NATION.'

Notice that this promise of a Kingdom of Priests conditional... "IF YOU OBEY ME."

One day, *when* Moses was on the mountain talking to the LORD, while down below Aaron built an false altar. He collected jewelry to made an idol like a calf (which was one of the gods of Egypt, from where they were prisoners).

How the Priesthood Changed

The people feasted with much celebration and sacrificing to their new Egyptian god. During their party, Moses returned to find their merriment and feasting!

Ex 32:25-26 Moses saw that the people were running wild and that Aaron had let them get out of control and so they become a laughingstock to their enemies.

Moses stood at the entrance to the camp and said, "Whoever is for the Lord, come to me!' And all the Levites rallied to him.

- Notice again this imperative point – only one tribe responded.
- The other Israelites forfeited their opportunity.

➡ Only the Levites gathered to Him. On that night of great rebellion, three thousand rebellious men died. The Order of Levitical Priesthood came from the rebellion of God's people at the base of Mountain of Sinai, and consequently, the Law was established.

"Then Moses said (to the LEVITES), 'You have been SET APART TO THE LORD TODAY'" (NIV).

- Remember, GOD'S PURPOSE from the beginning was to have A KINGDOM OF PRIESTS.

The Revealing of Melchizedek

- But, a substitute was born -- the Levites were not the entirety of God's first choice
- Firstborn of tribe of Levi became a male priesthood
- The Levitical (Aaronic) priesthood began
- This priesthood had no incarnation
- Daily sacrifices were demanded

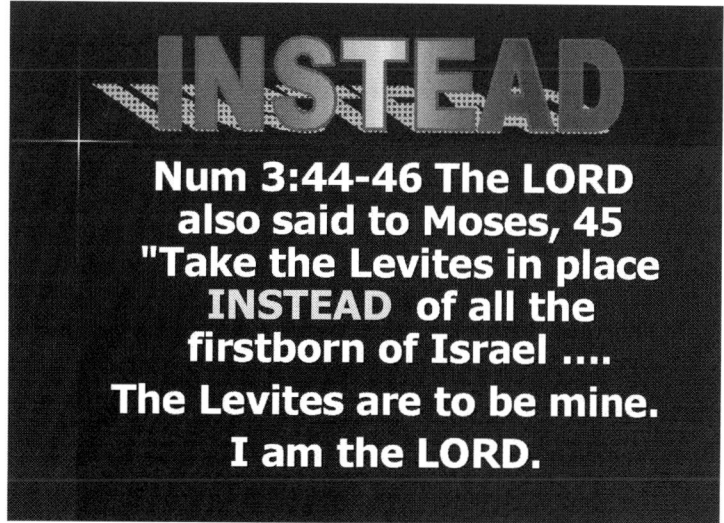

"The LORD also said to Moses, "TAKE THE LEVITES IN PLACE (INSTEAD) OF ALL THE FIRSTBORN OF ISRAEL, and the livestock of the Levites in place (INSTEAD) of their livestock. The Levites are to be mine. I am the LORD" (Num 3:44-46).

The Lord told Moses, "TAKE THE LEVITES INSTEAD!... The Levites are to be mine!" (Ex. 32, Numb. 3:44-46). Now... because Israel chose to not stand with God, everything changed. God's plan for Israel to be a Kingdom of Priest, was refused.

One must wonder why the present day church focuses so much on wanting to maintain their Levitical worship, ritual, and order. Why? This was not God's original intention. Jesus gave us "another priesthood" (Heb. 7:12). And furthermore, unless you were born into the Jewish tribe of Levi, you could never qualify for the Levitical Priesthood!

Here the Levitical priesthood was set up INSTEAD of the KING PRIEST model that the Lord tried to establish earlier.

LEVITICAL PRIESTHOOD	MELCHIZEDEK PRIESTHOOD
They were Priests only	Both king and priest
Based on the Law	Based on Choice
Based on Levite lineage	Everyone
No Spiritual Qualifications	Only Spiritual & Character qualifications
Aaron the High Priest	Jesus the Great High Priest
Physical & Age Requirements	Heart to love God
Table of Showbread	Communion Table
Law of Stone Tablets	Law on Heart and Mind
Without an Oath	With an Oath
Earthly Tabernacle	Heavenly Dimension
Created as a consequence of rebellion	Created as a Heavenly Pattern
Ministry To One Nation - Israel	Ministry To All the World
Blessings & Curses	Blessings
Ritual	Rejoicing
Weak & ineffective	Effective - Powerful
Temporary	Eternal
Continual Sacrifice for Sin	Once and for all - No More Sacrifice
Only a Select Few	Any Believer
Blood of Animals	Blood of Jesus
Basis of the Law	Choice
Physical Requirements	Heart
Endless Sacrifice	Endless Life

The Law was given to the Jew and not the Gentile.

God always wanted a Kingdom of priests.

INSTEAD. INSTEAD. This was not the original plan of the Kingdom of Priests! The **FIRSTBORN** son of the Levites became a **FIRSTFRUIT** tithe to the Lord.

- Now only MEN could be priests.
- But, not all men could be priests! They had to be born of the Tribe of Levi and descendents of Aaron.
- They had to be ages 25 - 50.
- They could not be blind, defected, hunchbacked or a dwarf.
- They could have no Injuries or skin disease.
- Having their testicles CRUSHED would disqualify them to serve (Lev. 21:17-24).
- They must have married a virgin -- one who was never a prostitute, nor divorced, widowed, nor raped.
- Each individual sexual act was considered "unclean" and temporarily disqualified their service.
- They had to be PERFECT physical specimens.
- They could not own land.
- They had NO governmental authority over their nation.

Of this select group, many often failed miserably!

- Often they were wicked (1 Sam. 2:22-25, 4:11),
- They didn't seek after the Lord (2:8),
- They didn't rule with God's authority (5:30-31),
- And they dealt falsely with people (6:13).

Obviously, those restrictions don't leave many of us to be qualified to serve! Now you understand more about why there was the necessity to change the priesthood.

If your actions and belief systems are still Levitical, everything else will be outdated with your doctrine. THINK ABOUT IT... Jesus never appointed a levitical priest!

"Therefore, if perfection were through the Levitical priesthood (for under it the people received the law what further need was there that ANOTHER (HETEROS – ANOTHER DIFFERENT SORT OF PRIEST) priest should rise according to the order of Melchizedek (A KING PRIEST, BEFORE LAW), and not be called according to the order of Aaron?" (Heb. 7:11-8:1)

- People were bound by legalism and law.
- The law was added because of transgressions (Gal. 3;19).
- This priesthood was "Weak, imperfect, and unprofitable.
- It was tribally based.
- Their continual sacrifices could not bring forgiveness of sin.

"Another of a Different Kind Must Come by Necessity!"

The Aaronic (Levitical priesthood) was established at Mt. Sinai (Ex. 19:6) and was brought to an end at the cross (Rom. 10:4, Mat. 5:17-18; Rom. 10:1- 4).

It was the death of Jesus that changed everything – a NEW dispensation. When the veil of the Temple was torn from top to bottom, it signified that the Old Covenant became completed and the New Covenant began.

Continuing with Hebrews 10:12 "For the priesthood being changed, of necessity there is also a change of the law."This New Day of understanding is upon us... and this verse is no longer a riddle! It was NECESSARY!

Jesus belongs to another tribe, from which no man has officiated at the altar. He arose from Judah (also the lineage of David), of which tribe Moses didn't speak concerning priesthood (vs. 13-14).

> This new priesthood from Judah arises out of praise... [14]NOT LEVITICAL. Jesus did not come to earth as Aaronic priest – He was from the tribe of Judah.

The old (Aaronic) was abolished – Jesus took away the first – (Heb. 10:9) to establish the second.[15] This Melchizedek Priesthood is:

- Not a special priesthood for a select few.
- Is given to every human (not just men, or men of one tribe).
- Not a clerical caste.

Jesus gave us His royal priesthood. It was called – Melchizedek! And this immense action moved humanity into a new covenant. Now you and I are ALL Melchizedek PRIESTS.

Melchizedek Was The First Priesthood And The Last!

"There was a NECESSITY that *another* priest should rise according to the order of Melchizedek (A KING PRIEST), and not be called according to the order of Aaron."

Continuing: Hebrews 10:15 "And it is yet far more evident if, in the likeness (RESEMBLENCE OR REFLECTION, PROTOTYPE) of Melchizedek, there arises *another (heteros)* priest."

- *Heteros* = another of a different kind.
- He was both King/priest at the same time.
- "Who has come, not according to the law of a fleshly commandment, but according to the power of an endless life."
- It was an endless priesthood!
- Holy Nation
- 1 Peter 2:9-10, *"But you are a chosen people, a royal priesthood, a holy nation, a people belonging to God..."* (NIV).
- Special people. Chosen of God.

---

14. Judah means praise.
15. Principle of the second (son).

- Royal – ruling and reigning with Christ, exercising authority in the Kingdom.

- Priesthood – offering the sacrifice of worship and a pure heart.

- Their assignment shows forth the praises of God in all that they do.

- To be the ones IN His marvelous light.

 It seems that the Melchizedek Priesthood was established by the apostles after the Ascension. Peter spoke of the PEOPLE (not just the Levites) being "a HOLY priesthood" (1 Peter 2:5) and "a ROYAL priesthood" (1 Peter 2:9).

Jesus Is BETTER

Continuing in Hebrews: 22 "By so much more Jesus has become a surety of a BETTER covenant. 23 Also there were many priests, because they were prevented by death from continuing. 24 But He, because He continues forever, has an unchangeable priesthood." This the pattern of unchangeable heavens.

Levitical	Melchizedek
Weak - stops at each priest's death.	Better - unchangeable. Endless
No governmental authority	The Government is on His shoulders

Jesus not only fulfilled the Old Testament but He is BETTER and His covenant is BETTER than those types and shadows that foretold Him.

- Jesus is better than Moses.

- He is better than the Law.

- He is better than David.

- Better than the angels.

- Better than the Levitical sacrifices.

25 "Therefore He is also able to save to the *uttermost* those who come to God through Him, since He always lives to make intercession for them, for us, who is holy, harmless, undefiled, separate from sinners, and has become higher than the heavens;" Jesus is not a mere human.

> He saves us to the *uttermost*! That word means final, complete and perfect.
>
> The preposition "the" is *ies*, a *Greek* word used when wanting to show "how far" the force of a word reached.
>
> In this case, the force of saving us reaches to the uttermost, to the final complete and perfect state of salvation. Our salvation is final, complete, and perfect forgiveness of all our sins. Without interruption...continuing as they happen...

27 "Who does not need daily, as those high priests, to offer up sacrifices, first for His own sins and then for the people's, for this He did ONCE AND FOR ALL when He offered up Himself." He gives us a FINISHED WORK!

Levitical	Melchizedek
Continual Sacrifice	Once and Final

The Melchizedek priesthood comes to full expression within Christ at His death. Since the time Jesus became our High Priest (Heb. 3:1), the Levitical priesthood has no need to function any longer (see Heb. 7-10). The need for it was finished!

The Levitical system of animal sacrifice continued until AD 70 when the temple was destroyed. Even then, it was an empty system of dead ritual.

Jesus ushered in the New Covenant, and with this Newness of Resurrection, He gave us His priesthood. As a Priest, "Jesus ever lives to make priestly intercession for you" (Rom. 8:24).

An Oath

28 "For the law appoints as high priests men who have weakness, but the word of the OATH, which came *after* the law, appoints the Son who has been perfected forever."

OATH = a statement or promise.
- God promised Abraham by swearing by Himself (Heb. 6:13-19).
- Melchizedek was a priest WITH an oath of eternal Priesthood.
- The Levitical Priesthood is sanctioned WITHOUT an oath.
- Jesus was made priest WITH an oath.

We are heirs of this promise confirmed by an OATH because it is impossible for God to lie. God cannot swear by anything greater than Jesus, Who gave us everything He was and is when we believe and receive Him.

Because we were nailed to the cross with Him, we died with Him.

We were in the mind of Jesus before the foundation of the world. Every word Jesus spoke, every place he walked, we were chosen IN HIM.

Moving Forward

OLD COVENANT	NEW COVENANT
Aaronic Priesthood	Melchizedek Priesthood
The Law written on stone (7:18)	The Law written on hearts (8:10).
Animal Sacrifices	The Death of Jesus
Temple in Jerusalem	People of God

The Melchizedek Priesthood has always been God's creational INTENTION for His people – to live life with a dominion (kingly rule) dominion (kingly rule) of internal alignment to truth in prosperity, wholeness, and balance.

Jesus waits in the heavenlies until the restoration of all things – He's waiting for us to come into His priesthood rule and domain over righteousness and peace.

It is not a priesthood of things to DO. It is not a priesthood with drudgery and routine.

God BRINGS US MORTALS INTO NEW PRIESTHOOD to achieve His purposes. The **STRENGTH OF MELKIZEDEK IS** for you and me **TO REIGN IN RIGHTEOUSNESS** and **PEACE**.

Can you hear the Lord speaking right now, "I raise you up now into My Melchizedek Order and Priesthood. Realize the blessing to be the possessor of heaven and earth. Be the King and Priest you are called to be!"

The "Order" of Melchizedek

"The Lord has sworn and will not relent, You are a Priest (Kohen) FOREVER AFTER THE ORDER (kata) OF MELCHIZEDEK."

We know by now that the Melchizedek priesthood was instituted BEFORE and remains superior to the Levitical Priesthood. Melchizedek was the first one designated *Kâhan (Koheen, Kohen)* which means a "priest." The first use of the word *Kohen* (priest), is found in Genesis 14:14-20.[16]

A *kâhan* priest was assigned to mediate, officiate, and execute the office, to be the principal officer.

- A priest mediates between a sovereign and his subjects.
- He intercedes and atones for the sins of a people.

"After the ORDER" (kata) is the priest's cycle of obligation. "Kata" means "after the fashion or likeness of."

The Levitical Order of priests were set aside to attend unto the ministry pertaining to the temple. They were assigned as responsibilities respectively in the temple to fulfill particular services or predetermined ministry.

---

16. In Hebrew, the word *priest* is used 26 times, *priests* 6 times, *priesthood* 5 times.

> Regarding Zacharias, "He was *chosen by lot* to enter the temple of the Lord and burn incense according to the custom of the priestly office" (Lk. 1).
>
> The Old Testament priests were in charge of many spiritual "secrets" that the people did not know. Only the priests were allowed to officiate in the tabernacle or to handle the vessels therein (Num. 18:16). They offered up sacrifices for Israel, and interpreted the will of Eloheim. The Israelites had to rely on the priest's testimony for any spiritual insights.

All of these secrets that were kept from the people were revealed when Jesus lived after He poured out the Holy Spirit. Then, the masses could hear the Spirit of the Lord without a mediator (1 Tim. 2:5),

> Jesus, being a descendant of Judah (praise) established a different ORDER of priesthood for us to enjoy.

The old order has finished its course,

 Peter (the apostle to the Jews, Gal. 2:7-8) wrote this important message to the Jews, "You (*who have been Levitical*) also, as living stones, are being built up a spiritual house, a HOLY (*royal*) PRIESTHOOD, to offer up spiritual sacrifices acceptable to God through Jesus Christ" (1 Pet. 2:4-6, NIJV).

Peter tells the Jewish people that this priesthood is for them as well, those who found it the most difficult to hear.

> When Peter wrote this, the old order was still in place.
>
> The Jews were being scattered in every direction.
>
> He tells them that Jesus is a KING and a priest.

WOMEN are part of this priesthood. Every race and class of believer is a Melchizedek Priest. **THIS NEW** priesthood is not ethnically driven. It is not class conscious or socially discriminating. There is no bond or free. Together we are the one new man, the new creation.

Through Jesus, the eternal ORDER of Melchizedek rules over all creation.

Aaronic – Levitical Priesthood	Melchizedek Priesthood of Believers
Under Mosaic Covenant	Under the New Covenant
Under Law	Under Grace
Priest to the Jew only	Priest to all
Born in sin	Forgiven of sin – Jesus knew no sin
Ages 25-50	All Ages
In earthly Sanctuary	Heavenly ministry
Made priests without an oath	Made priest by an oath
One Tribe (Only from Aaron)	New Order – everyone
Sacrifices daily for sin	One sacrifice for sin – finished
Only the High Priest once a year	Everyone can enter Holy Place daily
Blood of animals	Blood of Jesus
Covers but never remove sin	End to sin
Work never finished	It is finished!
A changeable priesthood	An unchangeable priesthood
They could not own land or do business	They can own land and do business
By reason of death	Because He lives an endless life

SECTION 5

Identity of Melchizedek

So... Who Was Melchizedek?

The identity of Melchizedek (*Melchizedec*) has been the subject of much debate. We can gain a greater understanding of the Melchizedek priesthood by learning what others in the past thought. Melchizedek's identity does not seem to be veiled to those in the early church to the same degree that it is to us. Perhaps because they had the tradition of their forefathers' teaching which was passed down from generation to generation.

Melchizedek could be both a name and a title meaning "Ruling Righteous Priest/King."

There are hundreds of legends and traditions about Melchizedek. We can only examine the more prevalent. Here are eight theories about who Melchizedek was:

1. A Godly Patriarch, perhaps Shem, the son of Noah.

2. A created person who was a "type" of Christ.

3. An angelic being or archangel. Actually Saint Michael as designated in the Book of Enoch as "the prince of Israel" and the Book of Jubilees (1:27).

4. A real person who is still unknown.

5. A manifestation of the Holy Spirit.

6. A Gentile King – perhaps a Canaanite King.[17]

7. A Christophany or Theophany of Jesus.

As we continue in this study, you will discover more about his identity. Although we can not prove exactly who Melchizedek was, we do know some about him.

Without Genealogy

If you read your Old Testament again, you will discover that almost every Israelite mentioned is given a genealogy – this man is the son of this one... etc. The genealogy of the Kings of Judah are re-stated. Very soon you get tired of trying to remember it all. But Melchizedek has no genealogy given.

To the Jew, genealogy was vitally important to the line of kings and especially for the priesthood. If a man could not prove his lineage, he could never become a priest (Nehemiah 7:64).

Genealogy is essential in the Aaronic priesthood (see Ezra 2:62-63; Ex. 29:9,29-30; Lev. 21:13-14, Neh. 7:64-65). Levites were forbidden to exercise ministry as priests until their genealogy was proven (Ex. 2:62).

Melchizedek had no record of his lineage. Hebrews 7:3 indicates that Melchizedek was "without father, without mother, without descent (*ageneal-ogetos*), having neither beginning of days or end of life."

> The phrase "without descent" (Heb. 7:3) comes from the translated Greek word *agenealogetos* which could also be translated as having the absence of a recorded or traced genealogy.

---

[17]. This concept was favored by Josephus. (Mentioned also in the Book of the Combat of Adam, p. 311).

"Genealogetos" means that a person's name is on public written record. Therefore, the "a" before this word (agenealogetos) means that a person's descent or lineage pedigree is NOT recorded or entered.

Melchizedek ruled over Salem (Jerusalem) and geologists think it was inhabited at this time by the Jebusites, by one of the Canaanite tribes that King David eventually conquered (II Sam. 5:7).

We can find this common expression in secular literature of that day to say that a certain person did not have a *recorded genealogy of a priestly lineage.*

- The genealogical descent of Melchizedek was NOT important, because THIS priesthood was not dependent on genealogy.

MELCHILCHIZEDEK	Jesus SON OF GOD	JESUS SON OF MAN
Without father	Was God	Begotten of God
Without mother	Without mother	Mary
Without ancestors (descent)	From Eternity	Descended from Adam
Without beginning	With no beginning	Born
Without end	With no end	Cross
Made *like* the Son of God	God and Son	The Son of Man
Abides as Priest forever	Priest forever after order of Melchizedek	Abides eternally at the right hand of God.

Unger's Bible Dictionary states "Without father, etc.(Heb.7:3) refers to priestly genealogies. Melchizedek is not found on the register of the only line of legitimate priests; there is no record of his name in that ledger; his father's nor his mother's name is mentioned; no evidence points to his lineage being that of Aaron.

Because Melchizedek is not recorded as being from just one tribe, his priesthood is not just for Israel -- but for every human being.

AGE: Age did not seem important to the Melchizedek Priesthood. Age was vital to the Aaronic priesthood – Levitical priests could not become a priest until they were twenty-five years old, and they retired at the age of fifty (Numbers 4:1-3, 22-23, 35, 43; 8:24-25).

Conversely, the Melchizedek is a priest for life and "abides a priest continually." The word "abides" in the Greek is in the present tense, indicating continuous action. This means that the Melchizedek is a priesthood of endless life that never dies.

Theopany

It is a dominate belief that Melchizedek was an appearance of Jesus pre-incarnate. This is called a theopany. A *Theopany* is an appearance of Jesus in Old Testament times before He was born (incarnation). A Christophany is also a pre-cross manifestation of Jesus. These words are often used interchangeably. [18]

Let's examine this possibility. Was Melchizedek a THEOPANY OF JESUS? Here are some examples of other appearances of the possible pre-incarnation of Jesus:

> Jacob wrestled an angel, and afterward it was said that he saw God face to face (Gen. 23).
>
> The Angel of the Lord appeared to Moses in the burning bush. When asked His name, He replied, "I AM that I AM." There the name of Jehovah was revealed to Moses.
>
> Joshua saw the Captain of the Hosts who told him he was standing on holy ground (Jsh. 5).

---

18. In the King James Translation, Micah 5:2 tells about many "goings forth." Many use this to imply appearances of Jesus, however it translates "their family goes back to ancient times."

An angel appeared to Manoah and his wife who ascended back to God in a flame of fire and they felt they had seen God (Jdg. 13).

When Nebuchadnezzar burned the young men in the fire, they saw a "fourth Man in the fire" who was "Like the son of God" (Dan. 3).

God sent his Angel to shut the mouth of the lions for Daniel (Dan. 6). And He was the Fourth man in the Furnace.[19]

Why Melchizedek Could Have Been Jesus

Melchizedek was the "priest of the Most High God," so he could not have been an appearance of the Father God. Many think that Melchizedek was the pre incarnate, eternal, pre-existent Word who became Jesus, the Son of God.

Throughout this book, we will talk about how Jesus fulfilled (became a completion of) every aspect that Melchizedek represented. But was Melchizedek actually Jesus?

One of the main reasons why Jesus is thought to be Melchizedek is because Jesus said to the disciples, "Most assuredly, I say to you, before Abraham was, I AM."

Jesus claimed to be the I AM Jehovah God who was *before* Abraham. Who else but Jesus could be without beginning of days or end of life? Who else could be greater than Abraham? To the Jew, this statement meant that Melchizedek was the greatest man that ever lived.

- Heb. 7:3 says he was "made like the Son of God" ("bearing the likeness of the Son of God," REB). He was "*like*" the Son of God which is a phrase used again later.

- Both Melchizedek and Jesus were a King and a Priest.

---

19. Eusebius, a 4th-century Christian leader and writer who is often called "the father of Church history," refers to these incidences as the "second Lord after the Father" (referencing Psa. 110:1-4; Gen. 19:24). And, emphatically clarifies his position: "But clearly they knew the Christ of God, since he appeared to Abraham, spoke to Israel [Jacob], and conversed with Moses and the later prophets as I have shown."

- Both have no beginning and no end (no genealogy).
- Jesus is also THE King of Righteousness and the King of Peace.
- Melchizedek served Communion that speaks of the Sacrifice of Christ.

Melchizedek	Jesus the Messiah
King of Righteousness (Heb. 7:2)	Yeshua *Adonai Tzidkenu*
King of Peace (Heb. 7:2)	Prince of Peace
Priest of the Most High God Gen. 14:18).	Great High Priest (Heb. 6:20, 8:1).
Both King and Priest (Heb. 7:1-3)	Both King and Priest (Zech. 6:12-13)
No Torah genealogy	The Eternal Son of God
Before Aaron (Heb. 7:6)	From Tribe of Judah in humanity
Abraham offered tithes to him.	Abraham saw Christ and rejoiced at his day (Jn. 8:54)
Was the King and Priest of Salem (Jerusalem)	Is King and Priest of Jerusalem and the world
Offered bread and wine to Abraham (Gen. 14:18)	Offered Himself as bread and wine to Abraham's descendents (Jn. 6:55, Lk. 22:20-22).
Greater than Levite Priests (Heb. 7:6-10)	Greater than the High Priests (Heb. 7:26-28).
Before Levi	Not of Levi
Based on Oath (Ps. 110:4)	Based on Eternal Oath

The Qumran "Melchizedek scroll" offers no explanation of Melchizedek's heavenly status, but rather takes it for granted. Many, including the Essenes and some of the writings in The Dead Sea Scrolls seems to favor the idea that Melchizedek was Jesus pre-incarnate. His mysterious identity may never be positively known for sure. Still, there is considerable evidence to think that Melchizedek was an appearance of the Son of God.

In the early church, certain groups of people considered Melchizedek as divine. Theodotus the 2nd taught the book of Hebrews saying that Melchizedek was the only other divine being besides the Father, was the Spirit who is identified as the Son. According to him, the Holy Spirit was what appeared to Abraham as the priest Melchizedek. Hippolytus is well known for publicly opposing this claim as unscriptural.

Not a Theopany

The strongest cases for Melchizedek NOT being pre-incarnate Christ are:

> Old Testament theophanies were appearances who came and disappeared.
>
> Hebrews 7:4 calls Melchizedek a "MAN." He is not referred to as an "angel" or as the "Lord."

The problem with Jesus appearing in human form was that He eternally existed as God and was not given a body until His birth on earth.

> When the Angel of the Lord showed up, there was always awe and worship. But, Abraham did not worship Melchizedek which is consistently done in previous appearances of the angel of the Lord.
>
> If Melchizedek (who was said to be a man) were really a type of Jesus, who later at his birth through Mary became a human, this would be a second incarnation.
>
> This Melchizedek was not called a "High Priest."
>
> Melchizedek was "made *like* (resembled, NRSV) the Son of God," not he is the Son of God (Heb. 7:3). "Made like" is the Greek Word *apho-*

moiomenos, not used anywhere else in the New Testament. It is thought to mean a copy or mode, being made similar.

Hebrews 7:15 states "And it is far more evident, if in the LIKENESS (similitude) of Melchizedek, there arises *ANOTHER* priest who has come, not according to the law of the fleshly commandment, but according to the power of an endless life." (The words, *likeness, another, second, and replacement* all seem to indicate it was not Jesus.) Here is the permanent REPLACEMENT functioning FOREVER as this priesthood.

It seems strange that Jesus would come as a *type* of Himself (Heb. 7). If the first Melchizedek were a *TYPE* of the one who was to come, and if the character Melchizedek REPRESENTS Jesus, then it makes more sense that they are two different beings.

Jesus never served as a priest on earth because He was not a Levite (Heb. 7:14; 8:4). It seems that Jesus was NOT a priest during His lifetime. He never appointed priests. But, He became The Melchizedek High Priest *after* he sacrificed His life and ascended to heaven. He now sits in His mediatorial role, (vs. 26) higher than the heavens.

"For the law appoints as high priests *men* who have weaknesses, but the word of the oath, which came *after* the law, appoints the Son who has been perfected forever" (vs. 28). This means this office was fulfilled by the Son in His earthly ministry.

Jesus did not come to earth as a priest! Although He currently holds to all three offices eternally. These were revealed to us chronologically. He came to earth as a prophet (Jn.4:44). He was announced as King in His first coming but was rejected (Mt.12:22-45).

After His resurrection and ascension, He received the office of high Melchizedek priest (Heb.5:6,10).

Interesting Shem Connection

Our Christian history and tradition has its roots in the Jewish faith. There are lots of Jewish historical documentation, rabbinical literature, apocryphal sources, and "Oral Traditions" that have been passed down through the centuries. We don't know what is reliable information on the identity of Melchizedek and his significance. But, these can provide valuable insights on what people believed at the time and what was passed down through the centuries. We have no way to validate them.

Please note that this research is presented as an "exploratory discussion" that I hope will prompt you to think through some questions for yourself.

Rabbinical literature claims that Melchizedek descended from the lineage of Shem (or actually Shem, himself). This is one of the most verifiable possibilities. If so, this lineage in itself indicates that Melchizedek was a human man and not a Theopany.

There are multiple references in the Talmud, Midrashim, and other works of Oral Torah that Melchizedek was another name (nickname) for Shem, the son of Noah.

Examples of Melchizedek being Shem:[20]

> "Melchizedek was Shem the son of Noah, a priest most high." (Pirke De Rabbi Eliezar 9A.i)

> "And Melchizedek is Shem, the son of Noah." (Rashi, Commentaries, Genesis 14:18)

---

20. For additional references to Melchizedek = Shem in the Oral Torah see also: 1) Jerusalem Targum on Genesis 14:18; 2) Midrash 126b; 3) Talmud, Tr. Nedarim 32b; 4) Martin Buber, Midrash Agada, fn. 18, p. 30. Jerusalem Targum on Genesis 14:18; Midrash 126b;Talmud, Tr. Nedarim 32b; Martin Buber, Midrash Agada, fn. 18, p. 30.

The Talmud says, "The title, 'Melchizedek' was held by Shem the *third born* son of Noah."

In the Oral Traditions and the Targums (an Aramaic translation and explanation of Scripture written after the return of the exile of the Jews). The Targumim (singular: "*targum*") were spoken and memorized stories that were later written down by the Jewish Rabbis in the common language of the listeners.

Melchizedek as Shem can be found in the Targums as in the following references: Melchizedek was Shem the son of Noah, a priest most high." (Pirke De Rabbi Eliezar 9A.i)

"And Melchizedek is Shem, the son of Noah." (Rashi, Commentaries, Genesis 14:18)

"And Melchizedek is Shem, the son of Noah." (Talmud, Tr. Nedarim 32)[21]

"Tamar was the daughter of Shem, [who is] identified with Melchizedek king of Salem, Priest of God the Most High. (Midrash Rabbah, Vol.2, Soncino Press translation, 1983, p. 796)

The ancient Jerusalem Targum in its commentary of Genesis 14:18 states that Shem was Melchizedek. Also, in the Midrash on Psalm 37:1(126b) Shem is referred to as Melchizedek who came forth safely from the ark."

According to many Jewish traditions (e.g., B. Talmud Nedarim 32b; Genesis Rabbah 46:7; Genesis Rabbah 56:10; Leviticus Rabbah 25:6; Numbers Rabbah 4:8.), Shem is believed to have been Melchizedek, King of Salem.

---

21. Caption on this photo: King of Jerusalem Melchizedek SHEM,3340,3432 son of Angel Gabriel NOAH (NUH) and EMZÂRÂ (NAAMAH), was born in 2454 B.C. 3495,3496,3506 and died in 1844 B.C. Google images

Jerome (the famous Bible translator) believed that Melchizedek was the Patriarch Shem. Luther also thought he was Shem (LW, Vol. 2, pp.381f). But, the truth is, we do not know if Shem were also Melchizedek.

Early Jewish Rabbis and major rabbinic tradition viewed Melchizedek as not being Jesus. They also equated him with Shem, son of Noah; cf. b. Nedarim 32b; Midrash Gen. R. 44.7; Targum Ps.-J. Gen. 14:18).

The aprochrypal *Book of Jashar* (aka *Book of the Upright*), specifically mentions Shem as being Melchizedek. The Bible refers to the "Book of Jasher" twice in the scriptures (Jos. 10:13, 2 Sam. 1:18). The *Book of Jashar* is the best-known of several "Lost books of the Old Testament" and adds some details to the Genesis events.

> "And Adonizedek, King of Jerusalem, the same was Shem, went out with his men to meet Abraham and his people, with bread and wine and they remained together in the Valley of Melech. And Adonizedek blessed Abraham, and Abraham gave him a tenth from all that he had brought from the spoil of his enemies, for Adonizedek was a priest before God." (Jasher 16:11-12).

Perhaps Shem and Melchizedek indeed may have been the same person. This would also explain why Abraham not only recognized him on sight, but gave him the tithe.

For sure, many wonder could Moses know such detail about all the things that happened so long before he was born? How did he write the Pentateuch with such insight?

Shem was on the arc. He witnessed – firsthand – the devastation of the Flood and God's judgment upon the world.

 HaShem (YHWH) is named as the God of Shem (Gen. 9:26). Shem's name came from revealed name of God, "*HaShem*" (See notes in index). His name meant "*name* renown as PROSPERITY."
(Hopefully, you see the connection here with *tsedeq*.)

If this is true, then Melchizedek was a PREDECESSOR IN THE LINEAGE OF LEVI AND HE WAS THEIR ANCESTRAL FOUNDER.

1st or 3rd?

Wherever all three sons of Noah are mentioned together, Shem's name was always mentioned first according to the position and sequence of the names, "and Noah begat Shem, Ham, and Japheth" (Gen. v. 32).

The Midrash states that Shem was Noah's first born (Ex. 19:7) (although many other documents say he was third born):

> Sanhedrin 69b "And Noah was five hundred years old, and Noah begat Shem, Ham and Japheth;... Hence thou must say that they are enumerated in order of wisdom [not age]."

It is thought that Shem lived from 2448 BC to 1848 BC. According to this dating system, he was born when his father Noah was 502 years old. That makes Shem 98 years old at the flood and he lived for another 500 years.

> Therefore, Shem was about 450 years of age when Abraham was born.

> Shem lived to be 600 years old and outlived his own sons. That means Shem lived after Abraham died.

It is commonly told that "Melchizedek" was Noah's "nickname" for his son Shem, and therefore, an early precursor to the priestly lineage of Aaron and Moses, the Kohanim.

Genealogies are not listed for absolute historical accuracy, but to show the line of God's leaders in the Hebrew nation over the generations. They may be fascinating, but not always reliable. Here is what we are told:

Shem was the progenitor (in the family line) of Abraham "Shem, Arphaxad, Shelah, Eber, Peleg, Reu, Serug, Nahor, Terah, Abraham" (1 Chron. 1:24-27).

> Noah
> Shem <possibly Melchizedek born @ 2448 BC

Isaac
Jacob
Joseph
Levi
Kohath
Amram
Aaron = First High Priest (Kohain Gadol)) <————
Moses

Shem actually outlived Abraham, who was his great-great- great-great-great-great-great-great grandson, by 35 years! Shem could have officiated at Abraham's funeral service.

NAME of SON	YRS. AFTER FLOOD-WHEN SON BORN	AGE of SHEM when SON born	YEARS LIVED by SON
Arpachshad (Arphaxad)	2	102	403
Shelah	38	137	403
Eber	67	167	430
Peleg	101	201	209
Reu	131	231	207
Serug	163	263	200
Nahor	193	293	205
Terah	222	322	205
Abram	292	392	175

Knowing the importance of Jewish family lineage, and understanding that they both lived in the same area, most probably means that Shem *knew Abraham well.* Shem and Abramham could have had a long father-son paternal relationship.

Shem (lived 1564-2064 years after the Fall) married Sedeqetelebab, daughter of Eliakim son of Methusalah. Genesis 11:10 says, "...When Shem was an hundred years old, and begat Arphaxad, Elam, Asser, Loeb, Aram, Gec, Hoel, Gheter, Mechec (Gen. 10:1, 10:21, 14:18-20).

SHEM'S AGE AT EVENTS & BIRTHS OF DESCENDANTS

- 98 years at the flood
- 100 years Birth of Arpachshad (Gen. 11:10).
- 135 years Birth of Shelah
- 165 years Birth of Eber
- 199 years Birth of Peleg
- 229 years Birth of Reu
- 261 years Birth of Serug
- 291 years Birth of Nahor
- 320 years Birth of Terah
- 450 years Birth of Abraham
- 490 years Birth of Isaac
- 548 when Abram's name was changed
- 565 years Death of Abraham
- 600 years Death of Shem

After the Flood

The Talmud says that Shem knew the great patriarch Methuselah for 98 years before the Flood (Methuselah directly knew Adam). Therefore, Shem had knowledge from the beginning of time. And he, Shem, was in the ark and experienced the Flood.

> Baba Bathra 121b Our Rabbis taught: "Seven [men] spanned[13] [the life of] the whole world.[14] [For] Methuselah saw Adam; Shem saw Methuselah, Jacob saw Shem; Amram saw Jacob; Ahijah the Shilonite saw Amram; Elijah saw Ahijah the Shilonite, and he[15] is still alive." The Talmud

The first chapters of the Bible quickly cover 1,600 years of human history. Noah, who was described as a "RIGHTEOUS MAN, blameless in his time (6:9) got drunk and seemingly engaged in some misconduct. The language here is ambiguous, but this is the FIRST MENTION of intoxication – (and it is after the flood). Ham did nothing to preserve the dignity of his father.

Shem and his brother Japheth were known for covering Noah's nakedness by walking backward to not look at him.

When Noah awoke from his drunkenness, he gave a fatherly blessing of peace and prosperity particularly to his son Shem. But Canaan was punished for not protecting his father's honor (in Genesis 9:25 -27).

> "A curse upon your son, Canaan! May he become the lowest of servants to his brothers. May the Eternal One, the GOD OF SHEM, be blessed, and let Canaan be his slave! May God make plenty of room for Japheth's family and give them homes among Shem's tents. And let Canaan be his (Seth's) slave also!"
>
> It was probably at this point that Shem received the birthright.
>
> This may be where the birth order was changed, and Shem is now listed as first born.
>
> Remember that Ham (the father Caanan) was cursed and Shem was blessed!
>
> One of the big controversies raised by this story... Why did Noah curse Ham's son, instead of Ham? Josephus argues that Genesis says that Ham had already been blessed, so he could later be cursed, son (Cush) Caanan was cursed instead.
>
> Japheth went with Shem to cover their father's nakedness. Yet, Shem received greater blessings. While Japheth was to be enlarged (vs. 27), he still had to "dwell in the tents of "Shem."

According to Rabbinical literature (about Gen. 30:6), it was Shem who offered the sacrifices on the altar after Noah came out of the ark. Also, Jewish Oral history says that this rebuilt altar was Adam's original altar in Jerusalem (which had been destroyed earlier by wicked people of the generation of the Flood).

Because of rebuilding this altar, Rabbinical documents say that Noah gave Shem the priestly garments which he had inherited from Adam. The Targum tell us about the custom for each Jewish man to pass his mantle to his sons and present to them their passed down priestly garments. Here is a comparative quote from the Taragum from Genesis:

> "And Malka Zadika, who was Shem bar Noah, the king of Yerushalem, came forth to meet Abram, and brought forth to him bread and wine; and in that time he ministered before Eloha Ilaha. [JERUSALEM. And Malki Zedek, king of Yerushalem, who was Shem, who was the great priest of the Most High.] And he blessed him, and said, Blessed be Abram of the Lord God Most High, who for the righteous possesseth the heavens and the earth. And blessed be Eloha Ilaha, who hath made thine enemies as a shield which receiveth a blow. And he gave to him one of ten, of all which he brought back."

Because Abraham was a direct descendant of Shem (Gen. 11:10-27, 1 Chron. 1:24-27), he (Abraham) would naturally have been in line to receive the blessing that Shem received from his father Noah.

Jerusalem

Judaism teaches that the first man, Adam, was created in Jeru-SALEM at the very place where the altar of the temple would later stand. He was then taken to the Garden. They teach that after Adam was expelled from the Garden of Eden, he returned to this Holy City.

In the early times, the Holy City was divided into two portions. The eastern or "Lower City" was called "Salem" where it is told that Shem lived and built his academy.

Moreh

The Scripture (Gen. 12:6) mentions that Abram comes on the scene in Canaan and he traveled to a tree! Genesis says he traveled, "As far as the site of the great tree of Moreh at Shechem" where the LORD would appear to him and announce, "to your seed I will give this land." So Abram built an altar there.

Abram traveled (*evar or abar* meaning "crossed over") from Ur to "the *great tree of Moreh.*" I've often wondered why Abram traveled all that way to get to a tree! Historical documents say that the tree was "the famous" place to come to be taught by the great teachers. Trees were often "school" sites.

> Deborah also ruled at the foot of a tree (Jdg. 4:4).

The Talmud says that Shem was/IS also called "the MOREH." Moreh (in Hebrew) means *"teacher."* When Abram traveled to the tree of Moreh, it was the site of the great teacher to learn.

The mountain of Jerusalem was called *Moriah*, "the place (home) of the Moreh – or teacher." From this tree Shem taught – and from this mountain, Shem ruled as king, teacher, and priest.

Mount Moriah is also where Abraham went to sacrifice Isaac, and saw the ram in the thicket.

> While talking with the Pharisees in (John 8:56), Jesus said, "Your father Abraham rejoiced to see my day, and he saw it and was glad!" When Abraham saw the ram in the thicket, he built an altar there and named this place "Jehovah Jirah" (or Jeru), which means "awe" or "God sees and has provided ahead of time."

Moriah was later named Zion (Sion), and it is also the place of the ultimate sacrifice – Golgotha!

Shem later built a city as citadel and he called it SALEM (SHALOM, or peace). Judaism teaches that Shem, lived in SALEM and there also built an academy (*bet Midrash*) to teach God's principles. The school also promulgated the laws current in those times. For 400 years Shem preached at his school in Salem.[22] He was said to be a prophet who foresaw the future glory of Zion – God's Temple and the redemption of the human race.

> According to Jewish tradition, many say that Abraham circumcised himself. However, most say that Shem was present at the *brit milah*

Interesting Shem Connection

(circumcision) of Abraham and Ishmael (on the eighth day, Gen. 17:23), and probably was the one who did the actual circumcision.

Other Jewish sacred writings claim that Abraham often went to see Shem at his school in Salem in order to learn more of God. Plus, Eber (Shem's grandson) also attended that same school.

Later, after rescued from being sacrificed, Isaac studied with Shem.

Tradition says that Isaac's wife Rebekah went to visit Shem regarding the struggle of her pregnancy and there was given the prophecy of the "elder serving the younger" (Gen. 25:22-23).

And when Jacob "stole" the blessing from Esau, he fled first to Shem's school in Salem.

It appears that all three patriarchs -- Abraham, Isaac, and Jacob -- personally knew Shem.

When Moses summoned Israel to prepare them to follow Joshua into Canaan, he mentions Shem indirectly (Deut 11:30).

 **Shem was responsible to govern that same area of the world that the Lord God later gave to Abraham as his inheritance. The Targums say that Shem received glory among men.**

According to Jewish tradition, when Abram met Melchizedek, Abram was fearful that Shem would resent him for killing his relative, Chedorlaomer. Whereas Shem was worried that Abram was angry over how Lot had been captured. They say the offering of bread and wine represented a "peace offering" between the two.

---

22. The Talmud talks about the "court" or "yeshiva" of Shem in the Talmud, in Avodah Zarah 36b and Makkoth 23b. Tradition indicates that Avraham studied in the yeshiva (Torah school).

 Bamidar (Numbers) 18:26 Thus speak unto the Levites, and say unto them, When ye take of the children of Israel the tithes which I have given you from them for your inheritance, then ye shall offer up an heave offering of it for HaShem, even a tenth part of the tithe. To them, it meant that the reason that Avraham paid a tithe to Melchizedek is because Shem was Avraham's Torah teacher.

Noah, Shem and Abraham also were all alive when there was only one language! All three of them all lived through the events and times of Nimrod building the Tower of Babel in Nineveh (Gen. 10:8-11). Several extra-biblical sources credit Shem with killing Nimrod, son of Cush.[23]

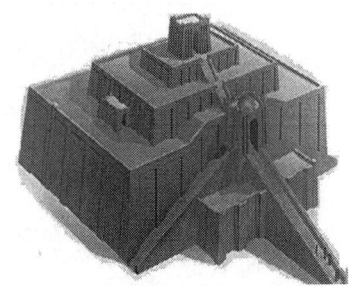

Shem lived at about the same time that Egypt began to build the pyramids and the Akkadian empire arose in Sumaria.

Luke 3:36 says Shem was in the genealogy of Jesus.

Rabbinical legend says that Shem ruled over 14 nations in relative peace. 26 nations are said to have come from him. The Jews, the Semetic nations, and even the Anglo-Saxons in Europe are said to be descendants of Shem. Also the descent of the British Monarch's are from Shem.

Jerusalem

Returning to the story about Ham's son Caanan being cursed by Noah, the Canaanites were in subjection to Israelites for some time, but eventually, the Canaan lineage conquered Jerusalem (Gen. 9:20-27).

> After Seth died, the Jebusites conquered and occupied the city of Jeru-SALEM for centuries. During that time, the city was known as "Jebus" after Canaan's son.
>
> After many battles and sieges, an Amorite king named Adonizedek conquered this city and built a false altar to worship Baal. His goal was to bring a return of Shem's great dynasty. Joshua killed Adonizedek along with four other kings in a battle in Makkedah. After that, the city became Jeru-SALEM once again.

Here's something else to consider: Eventually, Moses led Israel out of Egypt and into the desert. After they wandered around and received the Law and

---

23. Wikipedea

Levitical priesthood, and after Joshua led them across the Jordan, the returned to the very same land that Melchizedek ruled.

SUMMARY:

- Melchizedek's name means "king of righteousness."
- Jewish tradition identifies Shem as Melchizedek.
- Tradition says Shem reigned in righteousness.
- The inheritance given to Shem included the land of Salem.
- Melchizedek is identified as the King of Salem, who reigns over this same area.

Why Shem May Not Have Been Melchizedek:

Although Shem seems the most likely candidate, there are some reasons why it many not have been him!

> Why did Abram "sojourn there as in a strange land," if his ancestor Shem were already there and ruling as a prominent King?
>
> Melchizedek was said to have had "no end of days," but Scripture states that Shem lived to be exactly 600 years old (Gen. 11: 10-11).
>
> Moses wrote of Shem and used his proper name. If these were the same person, why wouldn't he refer to Shem as Melchizedek?

If Melchizedek were actually Shem (ancestor of Abraham), then Levi was also in HIS loins as well as in the loins of Abram – meaning Abraham paid tithes in the loins of one of his ancestors and he received tithes in the loins of the other (Heb. 7:4-10).

SECTION 6

Tithing

Melchizedek Tithing

Principle of Firstborn First-fruit

Giving to God has existed since the Garden of Eden. Cain and Abel knew what God expected as an offering. They both worshipped the same God at the same time. But Cain chose to give out of his predetermined self-will. Cain refused correction in the METHOD of his giving and consequently, "sin crouched at his door" (Gen. 4:5-6). So often, we're like Cain – "It's my way, or else I'll pout." His ATTITUDE was wrong.

Cain was the firstborn! He did give an offering! But... his offering was not what God required! Cain didn't want to cooperate with what God expected, he wanted to give in a "religious" way. He'd already decided was right (like we often do – Cain was tryin' to do his own thing and give in his own way). Cain's self-rule superseded God's will (Heb 11:4; 1Jn 3:12; Jude 11).

On the other hand, Abel's offering represented acknowledgement and recognition of the sacrificial intention of giving. His acceptable giving pointed to the future cross. Therefore, by faith, righteousness was IMPUTED to Able because he offered unto God a "more excellent sacrifice" (Heb. 11:4).

Able offered the FIRSTLINGS of his flock and their choice fat. The firstlings of the flock represent the *tithe* – or the fat: it was the increase of the best. This was the holy offering given to God that was accepted. Able's offering was a sacrifice properly given that had a redemptive effect for Able.

IMPERATIVE PRINCIPLE: The Lord is pleased with sacrifices that He expects.

Abel was obedient. Through faith, Abel was considered righteous BEFORE he presented his gift (see also Heb. 11:4).

The blood of Abel's sacrifice is a forerunner action to the forgiveness of sin and the removal of the curse that was to come through the sacrifice of Jesus.

God wanted the firstborn for Himself. The firstborn was to be holy to God. God expected more from firstborn Cain. Cain sinned because he did not give what was necessary. Perhaps it was the fallen influence of Adam that caused his oldest to fail.

Cain's gifts were not accepted. He pouted: Sin and the curse of it ruled over Cain (Gen. 4:5-7) because his attitude was wrong to begin with.

The First Fruit

The Lord always demanded the FIRST. The first of all grain and harvest, first born males of Egypt, firstborn cattle, herds, and flocks. Jesus is the FIRSTborn of many brethren. HE is the FIRSTBORN and the FIRSTFRUITS. "...the firstborn from the dead; that in all things He might have the pre-eminence" (Col. 1:18).

Jesus was the Lamb of God and the perfect One.

Midrash Rabbah - Exodus 19:7 says that ultimately, the Levites will divest themselves of the priesthood in favor of the priesthood of the firstborn. This will happen at the restoration of all things.

Principle of the SECOND

 IMPERATIVE PRINCIPLE: If the first fails, God takes away the first that He may establish the second. We see this principle repeated throughout the Bible.

Many of us pout and are disappointed – but we probably didn't make the right choices. The Kingdom is governed by Laws, just like the universe is governed by laws of gravity, etc. It does not help you to defend your mistakes and feel sorry for yourself – when the root cause of sin is not dealt with. Without Jesus, your faith and your sacrifice are unacceptable.

A few examples of the rejection of the firstborn are:

THE LORD REJECTED CAIN and chooses ABEL

THE LORD REJECTED JAPHETH and chooses SHEM

THE LORD REJECTED HARAN and chooses ABRAHAM

THE LORD REJECTED ISHMAEL and chooses ISAAC

THE LORD REJECTED ESAU and chooses JACOB

THE LORD REJECTED REUBEN and chooses JUDAH

We could go on and on. David was not a firstborn. Neither was King Solomon (who's name means PEACE).

How does this relate to Melchizedk and tithing? The old (and incorrect) has to be removed in order for God's New Order to proceed.

God never asked for second best or leftovers. However, many of the firstborn of Israel did not receive their blessings. They were unable to receive their inheritance and were replaced by the second. If the first son failed, the second was given first-born status.

Abraham had two sons.

Ishmael was the firstborn of Abraham.

Isaac was the firstborn of Abraham and Sara – but the second son of Abraham. But, Isaac was the Promise. "In Isaac your SEED is called (determined, reckoned, named)" (Heb. 11:18).

God sent Ishmael away so that He may establish the second son to get things in back in His order.

Why did Abraham have to sacrifice Isaac? Remember that blood was required in sacrifice. And… the firstborn is chosen of God.

Because Abraham offered the sacrifice of his long awaited firstborn son of promise, Isaac, he was called "faithful." If he had not done this, his faith would be lost – and we would not be heirs of his faith.

God provided a LAMB (Gen. 22:8).

Second Son Jesus

"The first man was of the earth, made of dust (Adam); the second Man is the Lord from heaven (Jesus)" (1 Cor. 15:47).

Adam represents the firstborn and because of his failure, death came. Adam was not able to walk in dominion (kingly rule), which had been the intention of Creation.

Jesus is the first and the last, the alpha and omega, the beginning of creation and the end – AND Jesus is also the SECOND Adam. (1 Cor. 15:45-49). He is both!

He was the only begotten Son of God, without sin and made sin for us.

Jesus (Emanuel – the God Man) was the earthly SEED of Abraham (Mat. 1, Gal. 3:16). Our natural man can't receive that of the spirit.

Our natural man must be crucified. We must reckon ourselves dead to this body of flesh.

Our new man is the second man or the spirit person that is created in the image of God.

Tithing

As you know, the principle of TITHING was established BEFORE THE LAW. Abraham (Gen. 13:2) gave to Melchizedek a tenth of the spoils of war ("plunder" – not a tenth of all his possessions).

The book of Hebrews says that a tenth (Heb. 7:4). He tithed out of VICTORY for winning the battle. Further, as we see, Abraham didn't keep these remaining spoils for himself. Hearing Melchizedek bless God for delivering his enemies into his hands, Abram gave tithes. The FIRST MENTION of tithing was when Abraham paid Melchizedek tithes.

CONSIDER:

> This tithe of Abraham to Melchizedek was BEFORE the Law.
>
> This tithe was NOT based on obedience to the Law; it was a response to a blessing.
>
> Abraham tithed out of victory and after being blessed by Melchizedek.
>
> We see that Abraham, the "father of the faithful," gave willingly and not under the law.
>
> Abraham voluntarily "gave" (not under obligation) a tenth; It does not say, "paid" (under obligation) (Heb. 7:4).
>
> His tithe was from the increase gained in war.
>
> We are not told if Abram tithed again.

Abraham's son, Jacob, also tithed 20 years later (Gen. 28:20-22).

Jesus, our Eternal Melchizedek receives tithes forever.

Tithing happened before the Law and then later commanded under the Law (Lev. 27:30-33, Num. 18:20-32).

When Melchizedek blessed Abram, the Aaronic (Levitical) priesthood yet unborn was in the loins of Abraham (Heb. 7:10) therefore tithed to Melchizedek. Therefore, the Levitical Priesthood (second) is subjugated to Melchizedek (first).

The tithe is holy and *already* belongs to the Lord (Lev. 27:30-34).

Who Received the Tithe?

Israelites tithed to the priestly tribe of Levi. There were also other times of giving designated for the poor, needy, and outreach.

Plus, at the end of every three years of farming, the Israelites set aside a tithe for the Levites, resident aliens, orphans and widows (Deut. 14:28-29; 26:12-15). This appears to be an additional tithe.

The enforced Levitical tithing was given to one tribe who descended from Abram by the rest of Israel (who also descended from Abram.

The children of Israel tithed out of mandatory command: Their tithe supported the Levites. **THE TRIBE OF LEVI WAS GIVEN THE TITHE.** Although the Levites received tithes, it did not belong to them. The tithe belonged to God. It was "holy" (verse 32), sanctified for God's use and purposes.

During The Law

For now, let's just mention a few observations. Tithing did not initiate, nor was it unique to the Hebrews. Tithing was practiced among many of the earliest people groups.

The Old Testament first mentions Moses giving the law in Leviticus 27:30-34 and Numbers 18:26-32. Tithes and offerings were primarily used to provide for the Levitical priests, temple upkeep, and the Feast observations.

Also interesting, is that the tithe was not always given in a form of MONEY – it usually was given in cattle, cumin, barley, etc. In addition to money, I've actually had people give me fish-head soup (with all the bones and yummy eyeballs!), lots of old jagged rocks, broken watches, coral jewelry, over a hundred pair of new shoes, new clothes, and a jalopy that barely ran! All the gifts were sincere, precious, and holy to the Lord.

Levitical	New Covenant
Animal Sacrifice	Blood of Christ
Temple in Jerusalem	Temple in us (1 Cor. 6:10).
Levitical priests no longer needed	Kingdom of priests)1 Pet. 2:5, 0)
Storehouse	Church, ministry
Flocks, herds, grain	Money, time
Specific lineage	Body of Christ Church
Guilt, compulsion	Cheerful giver
Robbing God	Blessing of giving
Levites ministered only to one nation	Melchizedek order of Jesus is to everyone

School Master

The PURPOSE of the Law is to act as our tutor, or "SCHOOL MASTER" that will lead us to Christ, and bring us justification (*tsedeq*, makes righteous) by faith (Gal. 3:24).

 The Law of Tithing was a schoolmaster – to teach us how to give while we are young.

The question is, "Why does the Church still need a School Master?" Yes, Holy Spirit should teach us! But... we don't all give as we should!

 Obviously, the church still needs a SCHOOL MASTER in this area. Believers have not reached a place of maturity and stewardship to be financially faithful without a legal requirement. THAT MEANS YOU SHOULD GIVE WITHOUT THE LAW.

BUT... if you STOP GIVING when you step out of the law, YOU STILL NEED A SCHOOL MASTER.

The Old Covenant is based on God's promises if MAN would obey Him. If not – God would curse him. In the New Testament (based on our new and better promises), God's promises are based on what He does – IN CHRIST JESUS.

When we graduate from school (become mature), we don't need a Schoolmaster anymore! We know how to live without constant instruction. God takes the lifeless Law written on tablets of stone and rewrites it IN our hearts. He pours out His Spirit within us to teach us how to walk in His way (Ez. 36:27-27). He covers the harshness of the Law with His LOVE.

Free From the Law

When we become free us from the law, we move into a place where everything we have belongs to Him. That never means to stop supporting the local church, the widow, those who feed us! That's our responsibility!

Jesus fulfilled the Law and purchased for us the right to surpass that rigid assignment by allowing us to enter into His rest. REST is creative and energized peace. Now our giving is motivated by the inner joy of release and freedom. The Holy Spirit can now interpret the fulfilled Law and blows away the exacting precise obligatory payments and strict adherence to duty.

Giving in the new covenant (having graduated from the schoolmaster) should be lifted up to a higher level than the Law. The Spirit of God breathes life into us concerning our charitable benevolence.

The irradicable Truth is Grace not works; Mercy and not law – these are pre-requisites to entering into the new and better Order. We, who live in this fullness of times, hold a better priesthood and we have continual access. Now, we can stand as a Melchizedek priest every moment before the throne of God. We bless others – and others can be Melchizedek blessers to us.

➡ Are you grown up enough to not need the SchoolMaster? IF NOT, YOU NEED TO TITHE. Do you give with an expectation of return? Then... tithing is the answer for you and you should be in bondage to a Law of tithing.

> YES – if you are unable to hear and respond to the Spirit of God to give beyond the Law when instructed.
>
> Remember, if you are under one Law, you are under all of them!

If you are mature, then your giving will exceed that of your childhood while you were at school. Are you a good steward? Then you know that love and giving are interrelated.

Benefits of Levitical Tithing	Melchizedek Giving
Opens the windows of heaven	Open heaven always
Rebuke the devourer for your sake	Victory over the enemy through Christ
Protection for your harvest	Fullness of blessing
Poured out blessing – IF they obeyed	Increasing prosperity
The Tree of Good and Evil	The Tree of Life
Pays to a Levite Priest to live	Gives to a King Priest to bless the Kingdom

The Revealing of Melchizedek

Are the Windows of Heaven Really Open?

Malachi 3:10 is most preachers favorite verse in the whole Bible! But if we take a close look at the verse, we will find something VERY interesting...

"Bring the whole TITHE into the STOREHOUSE, so that there may be food in My house, and test Me now in this," says the Lord of hosts, "if I will not OPEN FOR YOU THE WINDOWS OF HEAVEN. [24] And pour out for you a blessing until it overflows" (Mal. 3:10).

> Storehouse is translated "treasure house" in some translations.

Now look at this one: "And the priest, the son of Aaron, shall be with the Levites when the Levites receive tithes, and the LEVITES SHALL BRING UP THE TENTH of the tithes to the house of our God, to the chambers of the STOREHOUSE" (Neh. 10:38).

Look again! WHO is instructed to bring the tithe? The LEVITES! The tribe of Levi was GIVEN THE TITHE. Levites were NOT given land as their inheritance, as were the other tribes. God was their inheritance. But... not all the Levites were qualified to be priests! What is important here is that of that tithe given to the TRIBE of Levi, the Levites tithed to the LEVITE PRIESTS! Gave them THE FIRST OR TENTH of the TITHE.

- A tithe of the tithe was specifically held out for the Levitical priests.

---

24. See section on how the windows are now open!

- That first tenth of the tenth is called the FIRSTFRUIT or sheaf, or heave offering.
- The best of the best went to the priests (Aaron and his sons) only.

"Will a man rob God? Yet ye have robbed me. But ye say, Wherein have we robbed thee? In tithes and offerings. (9) Ye are cursed with a curse: for ye have robbed me, even this whole nation" (Mal. 3:8, KJV)

 This Scripture about "Robbing God" (Mal. 3:8) IS about the Levites FAILING TO TAKE CARE OF THE PRIESTS and causing them to labor for food!

Who robbed?

Who is cursed?

We saw how according to the Law, the Levites were given the tithe of the tithe for their needs and so there would be "MEAT in My (The Lord's) House" (Mal. 3:10).

Malachi does not rebuke the people, he rebukes the Levites for not giving their priests the best tenth (Firstfruit) of the Levite's tithe.

The CURSE of the Law

 Ever since the destruction of the Temple in 70 A.D., it has not been possible to keep the tithing law. Because that OLD priesthood is no longer necessary and the Temple rituals are gone the way of the cross, so have the Law of tithes and offerings ceased.

Therefore, Christians should not tithe out of the FEAR of being "cursed" (Mal. 3:9). Redemption frees us from being cursed - forever. Fear is never the correct incentive for giving. We live under the New Testament Law of grace!

 But hear this… If you choose to wallow in even a piece of the Law of Moses, you have a big problem… If you decide to believe in the LAW of tithing, you can not walk in fullness – because no one can keep the Law.

"Cursed is everyone who does not abide by all things written in the book of the Law, to perform them" (Gal. 3:10).

This Scripture is called a "Prove me" tithe – you have to DO something in order to OPEN THE WINDOWS OF HEAVEN that there might be MEAT in the Master's house (Mal. 3:10).

> THE TITHE IS A TYPE OF MEAT - we have understood it as milk, but here it is meat (see previous chapter on meat).
>
> The bodies of the animals (beasts) were butchered and stored in a "storehouse" (Mal 3:10). Malachi called this set-aside storage "MEAT" and that "tithe" of meat was given to priests as their inheritance.
>
> This MEAT fed the priests and their families, the orphans, widows, and strangers who needed help (Deut 14:27-29).

In the past, the Levitical priests needed sustenance that was provided by tithes. But, this priesthood is not existent any longer.

What we have to ask next is, "Does tithing still open the windows of heaven for you?

WHY?

Why do we have so many Church Conferences and articles about "How to Open the Windows of Heaven?" Do you really have to raise your voice, give money, and do all sorts of things in order to blast open the Gates to penetrate heaven with your prayers in order to see the power of God released?

A well-know (famous even) preacher said, "We can stimulate the heart of God to open the windows of heaven for blessing in our lives." Listen… it is not by personal effort! What a relief to know that a loving God chooses to keep Himself near. You and I are not responsible to open heaven! It is not by your might or your power, but by His Spirit that we can come boldly to the throne.

Seriously? Do your prayers open heaven? Can you plead, shout, holler, yell, sing, dance, or petition enough to get God to answer you? Do you have to tear them open? Why? Is God unwilling to answer you? And anyway, just how loud do you have to cry out? And how good do you have to be?

Some tell how Isaiah prayed, *"Oh, that You would rend (tear, rip to pieces) the heavens! That You would come down!"* (Isa. 64:1) You may have prayed this verse hundreds of times, but here are some questions to ask:

- Is the veil rent in the tabernacle? Of course.
- What does that mean? Everyone can now enter beyond the veil – into what was before the mystery.
- Did Jesus already "come down?" Yes, of course! Any questions? Did Jesus finish His work? That's what He said!
- Is the Holy Spirit always with you? Or do you have to cajole Him to join your meetings?

I hear questions like, "If the blessings of God are in the heavenly realms, how do we bring them down?" My friend, that's what Jesus already did! Believe it!

Faith is extinct if it is based on what YOU do (works) rather than what Jesus already did.

- Why do you pray for what you already have?
- Why do you pray for what God has already done?

Why not use this Scripture (also in Isaiah) instead? "This is what the LORD says to his anointed, to Cyrus ... **TO OPEN DOORS BEFORE HIM SO THAT GATES WILL NOT BE SHUT:** I will go before you and will level the mountains; I will break down gates of bronze and cut through bars of iron" (Isa, 54:1-2).

That same Spirit that raised Jesus from the dead does already dwell in you. He positioned Himself IN YOU, and that means YOU carry that same Spirit in your mortal body – you can sit where He sits. He knows what you will face and He ever intercedes. The Holy Spirit intercedes for you, and Jesus stands in the GAP for you.

The Revealing of Melchizedek

Be careful to not live in the Old Testament so much that you miss the power of the New! Don't just believe out of your own experiences! Change your mind – refine your belief systems – discover greater Truth... and you will see more happening in your life!

 When Jesus, the Pattern son, was baptized and the heavens opened (Mat. 3:16) and, the Bible never says that the heavens closed again! God the Father tore open the heavens because He issued in a whole new era of dispensation. He is HERE and NOW!

> Open = open wide, loosen, start, plow, to be loose, to be free!

You have the promise of walking and living in an open heaven – NOW. But, if you *choose* to believe that you live under closed heavens, then they are closed for you. Jesus said that the Kingdom of Heaven is within.

You have to believe! We as Melchizedek King/Priests rule under an Open Heaven. No demonic power can close anything that God has opened. If God opens, who can close it? And when He opens a door, no man can shut it (Rev. 3:8). Beloved, the DOOR is already open.

> Jesus said, "I AM THE DOOR; if anyone enters through Me, he shall be saved, and shall go in and out, and find pasture" (John 10:9).

> Here I am! I stand at the door and knock. If anyone hears my voice and opens the door, I will come in and eat with that person, and they with me (Rev. 3:20).

> If HE is the door, and you open it – then the door is OPEN. Unless you closed it, it is still open!

Acts 7:55-56, "But Stephen, full of the Holy Spirit, looked up to heaven and saw the glory of God, and Jesus standing at the right hand of God. 'Look,' he said, 'I SEE HEAVEN OPEN and the Son of Man standing at the right hand of God.'"

Like Stephen, can you say this out loud with me? "I see Heaven OPEN!"

This Open heaven releases treasures! The already open windows of heaven mean that spiritual communication is ongoing, just as it was before the Fall. Jesus restored us into right positioning.

The ALREADY open heaven provides the entrance to all that is new. The open heaven means you can do nothing to open it! It already is!

God doesn't need money! Not yours and not mine! He doesn't manipulate, coerce you, or make you feel guilty. He does not need your tithe because everything is already His (Ps. 24:1, Job. 41:11b). You give because it is the ever-flowing principle of life! God has already opened every window and will not close it.

Today, take what is yours… Align your thoughts to this truth! Be conscious and begin to delight in the fact that the Spirit of God dwells in you and become alert to the FACT that an Open Heaven surrounds you at all time.

Discover the intense passion of God's love for you.

RELATED SCRIPTURES:

When Jesus met Nathaniel, he said, "Hereafter YE SHALL SEE HEAVEN OPEN, and the angels of God ascending and descending upon the Son of man." (Jn. 1:51). It is possible to see it. Jesus referred to Jacob's dream at Bethel, when he saw a ladder set up on the earth, that reached up to heaven, and Angels ascended and descended on it. God promised to give him the land (Gen 28:12-14).

In Psalm 78, the manna that the Israelites ate in the wilderness was associated with the doors of heaven being opened (Ps. 78:22-25).

> "Then I SAW the doors of the Temple, the Tent of Witness in Heaven, OPEN WIDE" (Rev. 15:5).

> "I looked up and saw that HEAVEN HAD (*already*) OPENED. Suddenly, a white horse appeared" (Rev. 19:11).

SUMMARY: Tithing can no longer open the windows of heaven for you! The doors and windows are *already* fully open!

Wrong Ways

 You can make quite a good case for anti-tithing - the problem is that IF this information is mis-interpreted and many people will stop giving altogether. I've seen this happen over and over. And that is the LAST thing that should happen.

What we want to accomplish with his study, is to learn how to get out "from under" legalistic, coercive, and manipulative demands that try to leverage the guilt ridden.

Granted – Most of the principles of present-day tithing are usually based on Old Testament types and the present day superstitions. Unscriptural methodologies to obtain funds are never right!

Time after time after time, we hear well-intentioned ministries say things like, "If you want to know what your talents are (if you want your prophecy to come true, if you want your healing to happen, or if you want to be rich like me"), just give. And according to the proportion of your faith (meaning the amount of money that you give) shall be your reward of an answer."

Now, that's preposterous! We can't "buy" an answer from God with money any more than we can "buy" Indulgences (forgiveness) for our past sins.

Beloved, you can release your faith without buying something! Jesus recognized the faith of many who did not have to pay money to receive (Matt. 9:22, 29, 15:28, etc.). However, sometimes there were accompanying actions (i.e. take up your bed and walk).

We do not give just TO GET PERSONALLY BLESSED! Can we, like Simon the Sorcerer, even dare to think that we can buy God's favor? His gifts? Or His blessings?

Should We Tithe?

Let me clarify this section by saying that, as with most in ministry, I am currently dependent totally upon the generosity of people's giving to survive. That's the way ministry is structured for me... Although we never coerced anyone to give, we taught the standard of tithing and I personally lived by (and beyond) that principle all my Christian life.

Believers should understand that voluntarily giving is still a valid principle. The only place that a certain percentage is required is within the Old Covenant.

The knowledge of being free from the Law should cause people to give more. There is a greater truth beyond tithing – and that is generously GIVING what is holy, right, and good. But, wait!

 When it is all said and done, *THE TITHE IS THE LEAST WE SHOULD GIVE.*

Yes, the Lord wants to move us forward to where we are free from the law and begin to understand that everything we have belongs to Him. In the Old Testament 10% of what we have belongs to the Lord. In the New Covenant, 100% of what we have is His.

With that information can we question principles that have been firmly established in the church about tithing?

Truth is, Jesus talked more about money than any other subject. We should be able to discuss it without angry reactions. After all, our Melchizedek priesthood is about prosperity in every way.

Melchizedek Giving

If we, as New Testament believers, use Old Testament "types" to define the methodology of our giving, then many unanswered questions remain. Let's start by asking, what happened in the New Testament. Did the cross accomplish our full redemption? Is it a finished work? Or can we, by our actions obtain or earn further blessings? Do we have to DO something more to receive anything from God? Are we the inheritors of "all things"(2 Pet. 1:3) – or not?

We must clarify, "Do obsolete Laws ever apply to our life or our giving?" The answer is clear... Beloved, we are not under the law. Matthew 5:17-18 tells us the very words of Jesus, "Do not think that I have come to destroy the Law or the Prophets. I did not come to destroy, BUT TO FULFILL" (Strongs "*pleroo*" to make replete, i.e. (literally) to cram, level up (a hollow), or imbue, diffuse, influence, satisfy, execute, finish, verify, etc.). (See also Rom. 8:4, 10:4, Gal. 3:17-24, 4:4-5, Col. 2:16-17.)

But the principle of giving is not legalism... it is the Gospel. "God so loved the world, that He GAVE.

Because the law was FULFILLED, we find that the need for animal sacrifices was abolished, circumcision was no longer obligatory, and the detailed rituals of the Feast Days didn't have to be literally observed. Christ's sacrifice also did away with food laws, the Levitical priesthood, and the actual physical tabernacle/temple was no longer the only place for worship!

Jesus fulfilled and completed the law. He became our High Priest, our Sabbath, our Feasts, and our Sacrifice. He is The Tithe.

Let's agree together – JESUS DID IT ALL! He paid the price.

As New Testament leaders, we should consider:

> The redeemed/ransomed believer is not constrained by the rules and regulations of the law.

> Believers should not give because they feel they are provoked, manipulated, controlled, or made to feel guilty.

> We do not give to "get" a blessing. The blessings are *already* ours. The cross did it all.

IMPERATIVE PRINCIPLE: Giving images the character of God. The necessity of believers giving sacrificial offering is eternal (1Pet 1:18-20; Rom 12:1). The circumcision of our heart, ears, eyes, mouth, and our entire life still applies (Acts 7:51; Col 2:11). The sacrificial offering of the fruit of our lips is still acceptable. The intentional giving of our lives and of our possessions is at the crux of servanthood.

Each day is a brand new opportunity for you to be like Jesus to the world.

New Testament Giving

Tithing was the Jewish custom in New Testament times, because virtually everybody tithed – it was expected under the Law. Perhaps it was not necessary to mention it.

Pharisees tithed (Lk. 18:14) as under the Law. Jesus don't rebuke them for it, but he called them hypocrites because they were whitewashed tombstones (Mat. 23:27) and for being sticklers to the "letter" of the Law while missing the point. Their exterior was painted over, but they were rotten in motive and incentive for giving.

However, tithing is NOT mentioned as part of the New Covenant lifestyle.

Even though the Pharisees observed the Law of tithing, Jesus said they were "of their father, the Devil" (Jn 8:44). Jesus commented that their tithing lacked the "more weightier matters." They were particularly legalistic in their ATTITUDE about tithing, as well as their other religious ideas (Matt 12:1-10; Matt. 23:23, Lk. 13:10-17, Lk. 18:12).

Though He spoke a lot about money and giving, Jesus did not mention the tithe as being obligatory for believers who followed Him.

We are not told that Jesus ever received tithes, yet His ministry was always supported by the monetary "gifts" from others (Lk. 8:3, 9:1-6 10:3-16, Matt 10:1-10; Mk 6:7-11). And… He had his own treasurer (Judas).

Did the apostles teach tithing? No record. As far as we know, Jesus did not teach the apostles, the disciples, or His followers about tithing.

Did the apostles tithe? No record.

Did the early church tithe? No record.

The historical writings of the earliest Church Fathers does not mention that the early Church endorsed any form of tithing.

Was any New Testament believer ever told to tithe or give money to "get" something from God? No.

Did they give sacrificially? All the time!

Being empowered to give out of the love for God (and without defined percentage expectation), will usually result in a much greater amount than 10%.

We need to also look at the way the early Christians lived in the early church. PROVISION CAME to the leaders IN A DIFFERENT WAY! People knew to give. The book of Acts shows that even though people were NOT told (or asked) to TITHE, the minister's needs were met, the member's needs were met, and abundant resources were dispersed to the disadvantaged.

It is also possible for ministers to have jobs outside the church and to support themselves that way. Paul occasionally made tents (Acts 18:3).

Only some examples concerning the "living" church are as follows:

Acts 2:42-46 says that the Church grew and flourished. "...Selling their possessions and goods, THEY GAVE TO ANYONE AS HE HAD NEED..." (NIV see also 4:32-35). Now, this practice of "having everything in common" seemed to be a localized practice not mentioned in other places. But, the point is that the Spirit of God moved mightily among them and they gave unselfishly, generously, and without pressure.

Acts 11:28-30 tells how "...Agabus, stood up and through the Spirit predicted that a severe famine would spread over the entire Roman world... The disciples, each ACCORDING to HIS ABILITY, DECIDED to provide help for the brothers living in Judea" (NIV, see also 20:34-37, 24:17, Rom. 15:25-26).

CORBAN: If you have money that your parents desperately need, but refuse to give it to them in order to pay your tithes, you are doing exactly what the Pharisees did. You are saying your money is "Corban" (Mk. 7:9-13). Jesus said that action invalidates the Word of God. Another translation says:

> "And He said to them, 'You have a fine way of rejecting *[thus thwarting and nullifying and doing away with]* the commandment of God in order to keep your tradition (*your own human regulations*)!"

> "For Moses said, Honor (revere with tenderness of feeling and deference) your father and your mother... But [as for you] you say, 'A man is exempt if he tells [his] father or [his] mother, What you would otherwise have gained from me [*everything I have that would have been of use to you*] is Corban, that is, is a gift [*already given as an offering to God*]...'"

> "Then you no longer are permitting him to do anything for [his] father or mother [but are letting him off from helping them]. Thus you are NULLIFYING AND MAKING VOID AND OF NO EFFECT [THE AUTHORITY OF] THE WORD OF GOD THROUGH YOUR TRADITION, which you [in turn] hand on. And many things of this kind you are doing" (Mk. 7:9012, AMP).

All our actions should be motivated by an ATTITUDE of spiritual faith. Because we have been freed from the law of sin and death (Rom. 8:2), we are released into the law of the spirit of LIFE! Voluntary liberal giving is listed as a "spiritual gift" in Romans 12:8.

> Now, EVERYTHING WE ARE AND EVERYTHING WE HAVE BELONGS TO GOD. He deserves more than we could possibly give.

> The Lord desires a love relationship with us, not just a legal obligation.

Maybe 1 Chronicles 29 gives us great explanation for New Testament giving, "The people rejoiced at the willing response OF THEIR LEADERS, for THEY had GIVEN FREELY and wholeheartedly to the LORD!" This indicates that the people obtained joy as a "consequence" of seeing their leaders give.

A Change

Tithing was first adopted at the Synod of Macon in 585 AD, where compulsory payment of tithes (to the Catholic church) was demanded under the warning of excommunication. (More recently, the Catholic Church no longer demanded tithes.)

Hebrews 7:12 clarifies it by saying, "OF NECESSITY THERE IS A CHANGE OF THE LAW (a change into a new understanding and application of the Old Testament principles – such as circumcision, food restrictions, feasts, sacrifices, tithing, etc). A NEW PRIESTHOOD has come.

This "better covenant" exceeds the moral law. We move past doing something because we have to and into the place of wanting to do it. We move past the duty of giving under the Law, guilt, and shot-gun coercion – and into the Giving out of a desire of our heart. Our giving is not one of do's and don'ts.

1 Cor. 16:1-2 "Now about the collection for God's people… On the first day of every week, each one of you should set aside a sum of money in keeping with his income, saving it up, so that when I come NO COLLECTIONS will have to be made" (NIV).

> Here we notice that Paul advised believers of need, and then they prepared (in proportion to their ability) IN ADVANCE to help meet that need of helping people.
>
> Note that they didn't have to sign a pledge card concerning their future intentions! Their word was their bond. And, money wasn't always collected for a building fund.

Paul said that in spite of the Macedonian's extreme poverty, they gave in "rich generosity" that was beyond their ability. That giving was, "ENTIRELY ON THEIR OWN!" These particular believers thought it to be a privilege to share with the saints in need. They excelled in the "GRACE OF GIVING." Giving was considered the test of their love. (2 Cor. 8:2-11).

Notice particularly verse twelve, "For if the willingness is there, the gift is acceptable…" Paul was gravely concerned that there be a WILLING offering to provide for the "equality" of necessities for those in need.

2 Corinthians 9:7 "Each man should give what HE HAS DECIDED IN HIS HEART (in other words, giving with "no strings") to give, not reluctantly OR UNDER COMPULSION ('*anagke*' under constraint, coercion, or distress) for God loves a cheerful (hilarious, prompt, and willing) giver."

Gal 2:9-10 "James, Peter and John... agreed that we (Paul and Barnabas) should go to the Gentiles, and they to the Jews. ALL THEY ASKED was that we should continue to REMEMBER THE POOR, the very thing I was eager to do" NIV.

Galatians 5:22-23 makes it clear that the fruit of the Spirit cannot be regulated (even by an amount or percentage), because against such there is no law.

So... Now What?

Of course, the Law was abolished at Calvary, the veil was ripped. God no longer required the blood of bulls and goats or any other shadow or ritual that prefigured Christ. The ceremonial laws, practices, and customs were abolished.

 But, there is still an explicit MORAL requirement. The commandment against adultery or theft still stands. The Scripture never suggests that there is a nullification of giving!

So, if we don't give according to tradition (Matt. 15:3, Mk 7:13), what kind of giving does the Lord desire?

It's about attitude and purpose. We GIVE because it is right. "But to DO GOOD AND TO SHARE forget not: for with SUCH SACRIFICES God is well pleased" (Heb 13:16, see also 2Tim 4:6, 1 Pet. 2:5).

As we express our release from legalism, our openhanded generosity in giving should exceed and be greater than ever before. We express our covenantal relationships through liberality – knowing that the Kingdom requires money to accomplish great deeds.

To repeat, we are neither under the LAW, nor under the pressure of giving to "get." Be RELEASED to give freely, generously, and abundantly – far beyond ten percent!

GIVING	Under LAW	Under GRACE
WHY	No choice	By Faith, Cheerfully
WHO	Mandatory that everyone gives	All give voluntarily
WHAT	Giving first 10% of income, plus other tithes	Give liberally as Spirit directs
HOW	By commandment a duty, obligation, and Law – or be under a CURSE (Mal. 3:9)	Willing offering, to be a continual BLESSING
WHERE	To the Levites and particularly, the Priests	To those who FEED you and to promote the work of the Kingdom

John also tells us how to give, "This is HOW WE KNOW WHAT LOVE IS: Jesus Christ laid down his life for us. And we ought to LAY DOWN OUR LIVES for our brothers. If anyone has material possessions and sees his brother in need but has no pity on him, how can the love of God be in him? ... Let us not love with words or tongue but with ACTIONS and in TRUTH" (1 Jn. 3:16-18 NIV).

This is our New Testament model of responsible giving – where we GENUINELY LOVE our neighbor (Mk 12:31, Gal. 5:14, Gal. 6:2). Supporting those who hurt (*are in prison, hungry, or poor*) actually demonstrates our love for Jesus Himself (Matt. 25:25).

"Here (in Levitical system) men that die (mortal) receive tithes; but there (in Melchizedek order) He receives them, of whom it is witnessed that HE EVER LIVES" (Heb. 7:1-3,8).

Giving UP!

 Don't miss this significant TRANSFER/EXCHANGE. Abraham received a blessing, and Melchizedek received a tithe in return.

The Scriptures tell us three times that Abraham was "the friend of God." The Jews exalted Abraham, as the father of "the chosen people." Abraham was the covenantal pivot of all the Lord's redemptive promises and purposes.

But, here we find someone who is in a higher (greater) relationship. Hebrews points out that Abraham tithed to Melchizedek because he was greater! GREATER? We are told to CONSIDER HOW GREAT this Melchizedk was since Abraham gave him a tithe (Heb. 7:7).

> Genesis 14, "And without doubt the lesser person is blessed by the GREATER." Melchizedek was greater than Abram (Gen. 14:7, 3, 7. 11-12, 15, 17, 21).
>
> Melchizedek is considered "greater than Abram" because he was *AUTHORIZED BY GOD* to bestow this good blessing upon Abram.
>
> And... Abraham was not a King or a Priest.
>
> Abraham respected Melchizedek and gave him honor.
>
> People did not TITHE to Abraham the Father of our Faith.
>
> Melchizedek was a priest – he gave blessing and received tithes.
>
> Melchizedek was a king -- he ruled a territory.

If you can begin to comprehend something greater than Abraham, the father of our faith... then CONSIDER HOW GREAT THIS MELCHIZEKEK WAS!

> The Levitical system had not yet been established, and yet Melchizedek was able to authoritatively mediate between God and Abram.
>
> The Melchizedek covenant of tithing was confirmed 430 years before the law. This type of giving sets an example to all of us who are adopted into his family and receive the SAME blessing of prosperity!

Previously, Abraham was blessed of God Himself (Gen. 12:2). Now, he accepts a blessing from this Priest of the Most High God.

When Melchizedek BLESSED Abram, he blessed THE FUTURE LEVITICAL PRIESTHOOD that would eventually come from Abram! All of these are a "shadow of heavenly things."

 This action presents illustrates the IMPERATIVE PRINCIPLE OF UPWARD GIVING. "The lesser gives to the greater" (Gen. 14:7, 4, 11). This strongly shows us to give to those to whom the Lord has selected to have the right and authority to give us blessing.

And, support the five-fold person who feeds you – often, it's their only provision! Surprise someone. Be a blessing! Giving is the expression of covenantal Godly love to apostolic leaders and Kingdom ministries whom you can trust.

As we express our release from legalism, our open-handed generosity in giving should exceed and be greater than ever before. We express our covenantal relationships through liberality – We give because giving is an imperative foundational principle of life. We understand that the Kingdom requires money to accomplish great deeds. Surely, we can all agree that the church (corporately) requires substantial financial support for building payments, crucially needed staff income, missions, etc.

The rightful Church is not just one building, but all her ministers have the right to expect provision (see Matt 8:22, 10:10, Gal. 6:6 – an elder is worth double honor and we don't muzzle the ox). That's the way this system works!

WHEN YOU HAVE VICTORY, GIVE TO THE GREATER!

 Think of it this way – Abraham tithed into RIGHTEOUSNESS and PEACE. He tithed into PROSPERITY and Wholeness!

We are adopted as Abraham's seed, and we should give to those who are our Melchizedek.

Is it Okay for Ministers to be Paid?

We need to emphasize 1 Corinthians 9:14 "Even so the Lord has commanded that those who preach the gospel should LIVE FROM the gospel." Yes, we should support those who feed us. That means – hold on now – NOT JUST THE LOCAL CHURCH and that pastor, but to the 5-fold ministers, teachers, prophets, evangelists, and apostles who help you. Traveling ministries usually need even more assistance because they are typically not supported by a local assembly.

Finally, Hebrews 7:8 says *"IN THIS CASE MORTAL MEN RECEIVE TITHES, BUT IN THAT CASE ONE RECEIVES THEM, OF WHOM IT IS WITNESSED THAT HE LIVES ON"* (NASB). The point is: those who receive tithes should be those who Melchizedek leaders who have the witness that Jesus lives eternally.

King	Priest
The tithe 10%	The tithe of yourself

The only sacrifice is what pleases God – and that's YOU! You please Him. You give of your "things" as a King and of "yourself" as a Priest.

As we give under Grace, we become transformed because WE BECOME A TITHE. We give with abandonment - totally of the substance of what we have become. Oh, the glorious liberty of becoming metamorphosed into the Likeness of God. And, you are the TITHE – the best of the best! Your life is that willing sacrifice. You give yourself away!

Today, surely the Lord would say again, "Just as you excel in everything else... in faith, in speech, in knowledge, in complete earnestness... see that you also excel in the grace of giving" (2 Cor. 8:7).

The Connection Between Tithing And Communion

The significance, it seems, should not be missed between "communion and tithing." Abraham was given communion *BEFORE* he tithed. That means communion is NOT dependant upon giving!

- Abraham did not tithe to be blessed – he already was!

All this was before Abraham was circumcised. Abraham was justified (*tsedeq*, made righteous) by faith before circumcision (Gen. 15:6, Rom 4).

- God called this one time heathen on a journey to KNOW Him and that was not conditional upon giving.

Tithing represents the presentation of our earthly or Kingly things to God. Whereas Communion presents our spiritual self to the priestly work of Christ in the Kingdom.

- Every Christian should easily recognize that communion and tithing are both about gaining deeper covenantal relationships with God.

SECTION 7

Imputed Tzedek

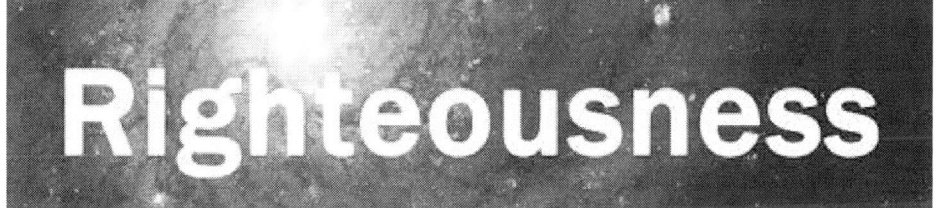

Imputed Tzedek

Imputed or Imparted

"Therefore IT WAS also IMPUTED (CREDITED) TO HIM AS RIGHTEOUSNESS. Now... it was credited to him, but for OUR SAKE also... and was raised because of our justification (, makes righteous)" (Rom. 4:22–25).

> Jesus was righteous. He became righteousness for us. "FOR OUR SAKE." He gives us His righteousness. It is already ours... We just need to realize it.
>
> IMPUTED means it is already yours and you can not earn it.

But, He alone is righteous - You can NOT DO anything. It's IMPUTED. You'll never deserve it. The Old Testament says that you are covered over with a robe of RIGHTEOUSNESS (Is. 61:10). The New Testament says that RIGHTEOUSNESS is within you because of Christ.

The Problem

The problem is the same one we talked about at the beginning – mis-translations. Somehow many insist on believing that their actions will appease an angry God. They think they can gain righteousness by doing something more.

These concepts developed into the ideals of virtuous and vicarious suffering. Saints throughout the ages believed that self-inflicted suffering would somehow impress their God. Therefore, they beat themselves, fasted until near death, and lived in austere remote caves. Extreme poverty was just another way to demonstrate their works of righteousness.

Some present-day activities (endless rote prayers, ritualistic warfare, obvious self-dying, etc.) "seem" righteous but they're really just religious. This self-absorbing idea that you can add anything to the work of the Cross is becoming a false religion of its own.

> Religion keeps you too busy and too preoccupied to build the Kingdom. "I *have* to pray more, I *have* to fast more, I have to do this." Truth shows us that we get to where we know who we are in God and *want* to pray and *want* to make good choices.
>
> Religion teaches you to escape this earth, while the Kingdom teaches you to impact this earth and change it.
>
> Religion is consumed with taking everything of this earth to heaven, while the Kingdom brings heaven to earth.
>
> Religion is about dying to self, while the Kingdom shows us the LIFE Giver! We have been given "a new and life-giving way" by the "Great High Priest who rules over God's house" (Heb. 10:20-22).

You and I must not strive for what is already ours (2 Tim. 2:24).

Paul talked about the problem of disappointment when speaking to the Israelites, (Romans 10:2) "For I bear them witness that they have a zeal (fervent ardor) for God, but not according to knowledge." Even though they have "zeal", nothing happens. "For THEY BEING IGNORANT OF GOD'S RIGHTEOUSNESS, AND "SEEKING TO ESTABLISH THEIR OWN RIGHTEOUSNESS, have not submitted to the RIGHTEOUSNESS of God." Their actions are "NOT ACCORDING TO KNOWLEDGE" (FULL DISCERNMENT) (Rom. 10:2-3).

> Here it is again! Paul was talking about the same problem we have today – many well-intentioned believers unknowingly "seek to establish their own righteousness." They hope that because of their sacrificial actions, God will respond.

You can NOT earn righteousness! "God made him who had no sin to be sin for us, so **THAT IN HIM WE MIGHT BECOME THE RIGHTEOUSNESS OF GOD**" (2 Cor. 5:21, NIV).

> God's righteousness is essential in His nature – as He is the only righteous Governor of all creations.

The righteousness of Christ was achieved by the Cross – a once-and-for-all, non-repeated action that took place externally from us. It happened because of the obedience of Jesus as He sacrificed Himself as an offering for SIN (Is. 53:10).

> "He [God] made Him who knew no sin to be sin on our behalf, so that we might become the RIGHTEOUSNESS of God in Him." Here we have a DOUBLE IMPUTATION. God imputed our sins to Christ who knew no sin. And God IMPUTED his RIGHTEOUSNESS TO US who had no righteousness of our own" (2 Cor. 5:21).

Christ voluntarily assumed both our nature and our obligation so that in our stead He could do for us that which we could never do for ourselves (see Gal. 4:4-5). This inward understanding expectantly embraces the righteousness of God and this becomes the central definition of our self-worth. We become the transformed **NEW CREATION** that brings the life of God out into the world.

 IMPUTED is NOT the same as IMPARTED. God "imparts" Gifts to us that grow. We can come into agreement with those Gifts that are exercised by being used.

> *Impartation Can Grow Through Our Cooperation And Faith.*

But, Righteousness is IMPUTED – it is IN our account because of Christ! IN the revelation of HIM, we can understand God's great IMPUTATION!

> God imputed sin to Christ who knew no sin.
>
> God imputes righteousness to us.
>
> We have nothing to do with imputation – it just IS.

Because RIGHTEOUSNESS is imputed, it is already yours! "Christ Jesus...has become FOR US wisdom from God - that is, our RIGHTEOUSNESS, holiness and redemption" (1 Cor.1:30 NIV).

Righteousness is IMPUTED to you whether you believe it or not. Righteousness has to do with God's gift of LIFE through Christ. IMPARTATION is subjective – that means it is totally apart from any human participation. It is apart from the law (Rom. 3:21 – meaning it is not part of works of law-keeping.) We have no part in it – except to perceive what is ours.

IT'S FREE and you don't deserve it! This is what Christ came to do: He *fulfills all righteousness* (Mat. 3:15) and died a death that would remove all your sins and become for you a perfect RIGHTEOUSNESS.

This present world will be impacted by the manifested life-giving forces of transformed believers.

> As you access the benefits of Salvation, you discover that it hinges on the fullness of righteousness. Righteousness is what Melchizedek reveals.
>
> Ezekiel broke old doctrine by saying that a RIGHTOUS man could NOT be held accountable or suffer because of his ancestor's (forefather's) sins (Ex. 18:20).

"Establish your heart in righteousness, and you shall be far from oppression for you shall not fear, and from terror for it shall not come near you" (Isa 54:14).

Galatians 2:21 warns us that our righteousness only comes because of Him... "For if righteousness could be gained through the law, (our fastings, our works, our pleading, our efforts, our struggles, or our sincere need) CHRIST DIED FOR NOTHING!" NIV. If we think we can do something more, we crucify Him once again!

Stop trying to please God with the carnality of your wretched lives. It's time to wake up and LIVE fully – realizing that Jesus ALREADY GAVE IT ALL to you and me! You can only gain your RIGHTEOUSNESS and all that it entails by renewing your mind.

In interpreting truth, we must remember that the greatest surrender is to become aware of what God has already done! It is FINISHED and when we surrender of religious notions about having to EARN something, we attain our highest destiny.

Having the faith to believe yourselves to be righteous maximizes your life.

Righteousness By Faith

"By MY RIGHTEOUSNESS, one will live by FAITH. And I take no pleasure in the one who shrinks back. But we... are those who have faith and are saved." (Heb. 10:38).

Faith unites you with Jesus when the realization totally comes that Jesus is righteousness IN you and for YOU!

This Scripture leaped off the pages for me when studying this topic: "This righteousness from God COMES THROUGH FAITH in Jesus Christ TO ALL who believe. There is NO DIFFERENCE... (we) are justified (acquitted to obtain righteousness) freely by his grace (the divine influence on the heart) through the redemption (ransom in full) that came by Christ Jesus" (Rom 3:22-25 NIV). It's a done deal!

> Not only for us from first to last, but for all God's people, "Righteousness begins and ends with faith" (Rom. 22-25, NCV).
>
> The COMPREHENSION OF RIGHTEOUSNESS IS PROGRESSIVE – it only comes by faith and develops as our faith matures. We go from glory to glory.

Paul warned them to not try to be righteous by their own works of following the Law. In fact, he renounces various attempts of trying to make himself right with God, instead of relying on Divine grace. "I have suffered the loss of all things and count them as rubbish, in order that I may gain Christ and be found in him, not having a righteousness of my own that comes from the law, but that which comes through faith in Christ, the RIGHTEOUSNESS FROM GOD THAT DEPENDS ON FAITH" (Phil. 3:7-9).

If you are a Melchizedek King Priest, your RULE will be over Righteousness! Our faith brings us into this *awareness*. "For in it (the Gospel of Christ) the RIGHTEOUSNESS of God is revealed from FAITH TO FAITH; as it is written, "The just shall live by faith." (Rom. 1:17, NKJV).

ABRAHAM: Romans 4:18-25 tells us that Abraham in hope believed, against all hope... and without weakening in his faith, he faced the FACT that his body was as good as dead... Yet he did not waver through unbelief regarding the promise of God... being fully persuaded that God had power to do what he had promised... This is why his FAITH "WAS CREDITED (counted, reckoned, considered, reputed, added to our account) TO HIM AS RIGHTEOUSNESS" (4:22).

> Abraham was not perfect! He made many mistakes! But, he was counted righteous simply because of his FAITH in the Divine Promise.

> **ABRAM - ABRAHAM**
>
> - All families of earth blessed (Gen. 12:3)
> - And IF you belong to Christ, then you are Abraham's descendants, HEIRS according to the promise (Gal. 3:29)

Because of FAITH when Abram was 100 years old, he was told that his seed would cause all the nations of the earth to be blessed. And he staggered not. Nothing was impossible!

When we "WORK" (toil, strive), our wages are credited NOT of grace but out of "OBLIGATION" (a debt). But for those who "trust God," their faith is "credited to as righteousness" (Rom. 4:4).

Romans goes on to say, "it was credited to him... but ALSO FOR US, to whom God will CREDIT righteousness, for US WHO BELIEVE in him who RAISED Jesus our Lord from the dead" (vs. 23-24).

When God sees FAITH, He sees your union with Christ, therefore, He sees the RIGHTEOUSNESS of Christ. That's how faith is counted as righteousness.

Take note of this process: (Step one, verse 25), "He (Jesus) was delivered over to death for our sins and was (step two) raised to life for (literally BECAUSE of) our JUSTIFICATION (the act of pronouncing righteous, or acquittal from guilt)."

1. He died for our sins

2. He rose for our justification of righteousness.

3. It is called the righteousness of God, because God provided it – the *dikaiosune* – from God.

This idea of FAITH bringing about righteousness first started to be understood during the first Reformation and Martin Luther. Rome considered the idea of FAITH bringing righteousness to be subversive to the Church and this is the major reason why they protested Protestantism. Of course, we have a much greater understanding now.

John Bunyan, the writer of Pilgrim's Progress, struggled terribly with this concept. When he came to a settled faith in Christ, he wonderfully wrote:

> *One day as I was passing into the field... this sentence fell upon my soul. 'Thy righteousness is in heaven.' And methought, withal, I saw with the eyes of my soul Jesus Christ at God's right hand; there, I say, was my righteousness; so that wherever I was, or whatever I was doing, God could not say of me, he wants [lacks] my righteousness ... I also saw, moreover, that it was not my good frame of heart that made my righteousness better, nor yet my bad frame that made my righteousness worse, for my righteousness was Jesus Christ himself... Righteousness (by faith) leads to life....*
>
> *Now did my chains fall off my legs indeed. I was loosed from my afflictions and irons; my temptations also fled away; so that from that time those dreadful scriptures of God left off to trouble me; now went I also home rejoicing for the grace and love of God. (John Bunyan, Grace Abounding to the Chief of Sinners.*[25]

Romans 10:4 - The Righteousness of FAITH

> **"For Christ is the END OF THE LAW FOR RIGHTEOUSNESS TO EVERYONE WHO BELIEVES"** (Rom. 10:4).

This verse above means that if you believe, you have righteousness because Christ is the end of the law.

> Jesus is the END OF THE LAW. That word, "end" is a very important word that "*tells*" which means to set out for a definite point, or goal, or a limit. The resurrection of Christ became the definite goal, the limit (or fulfillment) of the Law.

---

25. [Hertfordshire: Evangelical Press, 1978, orig. 1666], pp. 90-91)

The law required total obedience (Rom 3:10, 19, 20; 8:4). The death and life of Jesus totally redeemed humanity from the futile works of self and trying to please God. Jesus pleased God FOR US. With His perfectly effective self-sacrificing love (John 3:16), He fully accomplished our righteousness for us.

Now, let's notice those two steps in Romans 4:25, *"He was delivered* (surrendered, step # 1) *over to death for our sins* (*paraptoma*, past wrongs – both unintentional error and willful transgression) and...

(Step #2) was RAISED to LIFE for (literally because of) our JUSTIFICATION (made righteous)."

- Everything that was necessary to obtain our forgiveness from sin was accomplished in the death of Christ.
- But, it was the resurrection into God LIFE that completed it all. Resurrection was the counterpart action that produced our JUSTIFICATION (makes righteous).

Righteousness restores us to the likeness that Adam forfeited in the Garden.

This #2 step is brought forth again in Romans 5:10. (Step #1), the death of Jesus reconciled us to God (in the Spirit man), (step #2) and His LIFE saves us (causes our soul to become WHOLE).

God "justifies" (makes righteous) the believer because of Christ's free gift of LIFE. "How much more will those who receive God's abundant provision of grace and of the GIFT of righteousness REIGN IN LIFE through the one man, Jesus Christ" (Rom. 5:17).

> Our purpose is to REIGN IN LIFE - not always trying to die to that old carnal nature. (I already died with Him and have risen with Him by faith. Col 2:12)

(5:18) "Consequently... so also the result of one act of RIGHTEOUSNESS was justification (makes righteous) that BRINGS LIFE FOR ALL MEN..."

Romans 10:5

Now that we understand that it's up to the believer to recognize RIGHTEOUSNESS as part of his/her new lifestyle character, let's return to Romans 10, and re-look at some of the Scriptures we've known for a long time now mean so much more.

Romans 10:5, "For Moses writes about the righteousness which is of the law, The man who does those things shall live by them." In other words, if we obtain our RIGHTEOUSNESS according to the law, it is determined by our own works and we'll never arrive... and we'll live in failure. If it is up to us, we'll never find it.

Verse 6, "But the RIGHTEOUSNESS OF FAITH speaks in this way, "Do NOT SAY in your heart (cardia, thoughts, feelings, internal knower), 'Who will ascend into heaven?' (that is, to bring Christ down from above)" This means, don't look for Jesus to suddenly arrive from heaven so that you can escape someday soon - to that great rocking chair in the sky - when finally you'll find righteousness.

> The effect of Faith is Righteous = conformity to the character of God.
>
> Abram was not righteous, but he trusted Him, and that faith was accepted as.
>
> So here is the great truth that faith is rightly regarded as righteous. Faith unites us with Christ, Who is our Righteous.
>
> Faith is the currency of the Kingdom. Faith cannot fully operate under the law (Rom. 4:14).

And DON'T say, (verse 7) "'Who will descend into the abyss?' "(that is, to bring Christ up from the dead)." Those who have the faith know they are already righteous! They don't have to sit around and wait for Jesus to come back a second time in the flesh to make everyone righteous.

Verse 8, "But what does it (THE RIGHTEOUSNESS OF FAITH) say? "The word is near you, in your MOUTH and in your HEART" (that is, the word of faith which we preach):"

- The word (*rhema*) is near you (closer than arms length).

- The (audible) word is in your mouth

- The word is in your heart (cardia, thoughts, feelings, mind, soul).

SALVATION: (#1 –verse 8) "That if you **CONFESS** (*homologia*, speak out loud the same thing as God) with your **MOUTH** the Lord Jesus." (vs. 10) "And with the **MOUTH CONFESSION** (*homologia*) is made unto salvation (*soteria*, delivered and rescued)."

Confession of your mouth (physical body) forgives and delivers you from sin.

By sincerely confessing our trust in Him, we are declared legally "justified" (i.e., made righteous, "just-if-I'd" never sinned).

SAVED: (#2 – Vs. 8) "And **BELIEVE** in your **HEART** (*cardia*, thoughts, feelings, mind, soul) that God has **RAISED** Him from the dead, you will be **SAVED** (Strongs # 4982 *sozo*, meaning to be complete, whole, and protected).

Belief in your heart causes you to be whole.

NOTICE: (Vs. 10) For with the **HEART** (soul,[26] thoughts, feelings, mind) one believes unto **RIGHTEOUSNESS**."

Belief (faith) brings righteousness.

---

26. See author's book, "Whole & Holy" for the understanding of heart being soul.

> Here again is the consistent theme that the believer decides with his/her soul realm thoughts, feelings, and mind to "Believe unto righteousness."
>
> That means you believe what the Word says about yourself. You are righteous. That's not arrogance, a lack of humility, or putting myself above another... believing God's word that is near is the only way to succeed.
>
> This process is how you progress into your Melchizedek priesthood!

Verse 11, "For the Scripture says, 'Whoever believes on Him will not be put to shame.'" (A hallelujah shout goes here!) When I know who I am in Christ, He'll not embarrass me. I don't have to grovel for His approval. I don't have to beg for Him to show up... He's right here. Obedience is no longer an arduous task, but a passionate desire of a righteous person.

Verse 12, "For there is NO DISTINCTION between Jew and Greek, for the same Lord over all is RICH to all who call upon Him." It doesn't matter who you are (Gal. 3:28), the Lord is "rich" (prosperous, *tzedeq* principle) to all.

Verse 13, "For whoever (that's you and me) calls (out loud with a word of understanding) on the name of the LORD (*kurios* supreme in authority) shall be saved (sozo, made WHOLE)" NKJV.

Now, we are no longer without knowledge (Rm. 10:2), we have understanding in our words.

Attaining your righteousness consciousness becomes the vehicle to achieving the replication of God's likeness – your wholeness.

Righteousness & Glory

Righteousness is also connected to GLORY. Glory = the resulting substance that shines forth because of a passionate on-going and co-existing encounter with the presence of God. (2 Cor. 4:6, 1 Ths. 5:23).

The consequence of RIGHTEOUSNESS is the GLORY! The radiance of God – the showing forth OF WHO YOU ARE INSIDE to the OUTSIDE!

> Ps. 97:6 "The heavens declare His RIGHTEOUSNESS, And all the peoples see His GLORY" (NKJV).
>
> Prov 16:31 "The silver-haired head is a crown of GLORY, If it is found in the way of RIGHTEOUSNESS" (NKJV).
>
> Isa. 58:8 "Then your light shall break forth like the morning, Your healing shall spring forth speedily, And your RIGHTEOUSNESS shall go before you; The GLORY of the LORD shall be your rear guard" (NKJV).
>
> Isa. 62:2 "The Gentiles shall see your RIGHTEOUSNESS and all kings your GLORY. You shall be called by a new name, which the mouth of the LORD will name" (NKJV).
>
> 2 Cor. 3:9 "For if the ministry of condemnation had GLORY, the ministry of RIGHTEOUSNESS exceeds much more in GLORY" (NKJV).

Righteousness Expanded

Right now it is time to be magnetically pulled into the NEXT LEVEL OF CONSCIOUSNESS. The majority of your SPIRITUAL WARFARE needs to occur withIN YOUR MIND - in order for you to obtain YOUR promised INHERITANCE NOW!

The revelation of righteousness involves having integrity and dealing rightly with others according to God's will and action. Please read these verses again now that you have gained greater insight!

> "You are covered over with a robe of righteousness that Jesus gives! (Is. 61:10)
>
> "I put on RIGHTEOUSNESS, and it clothed me; My JUSTICE was like a robe and a turban." (Job 29:14, NKJV).

"The LORD reigns; Let the earth rejoice; Let the multitude of isles be glad! Clouds and darkness surround Him; RIGHTEOUSNESS and JUSTICE are the foundation of His throne. A fire goes before Him, And burns up His enemies round about. His lightnings light the world; The earth sees and trembles. The mountains melt like wax at the presence of the LORD, At the presence of the Lord of the whole earth. The heavens declare His RIGHTEOUSNESS, And all the peoples see His glory" (Ps. 97:1-6).

"Behold, a king shall reign in RIGHTEOUSNESS, and his rulers rule with justice, and a man shall be a refuge from the wind and a shelter from the tempest, like streams of water in a dry ground, like the shade of a great rock in a weary land." (Isa. 32:1-2).

***

"But of the Son He says, 'THY THRONE, O GOD, IS FOREVER AND EVER, AND THE RIGHTEOUS SCEPTER IS THE SCEPTER OF HIS KINGDOM'...But to which of the angels has He ever said, 'Sit at my right hand, until I make thine enemies a footstool for thy feet'" (Ps. 110:1, Heb. 1:8, 13). The rule is with a righteous scepter. All enemies were conquered at the Cross. Nobody else sits in that seat of honor.

"We give no offense in anything, that our ministry may not be blamed. But in all things we commend ourselves as ministers of God: in much patience, in tribulations, in needs, in distresses, in stripes, in imprisonments, in tumults, in labors, in sleeplessness, in fastings; by purity, by knowledge, by long suffering, by kindness, by the Holy Spirit, by sincere love, by the word of truth, by the power of God, by the armor of RIGHTEOUSNESS on the right hand and on the left..." (Cor. 6:3-10).

The man who trusts in Christ becomes "the RIGHTEOUSNESS of God in Him" (2 Cor 5:21). BLESSED are those who HUNGER AND THIRST AFTER RIGHTEOUSNESS (Mat. 5:6).

"So now present your members as slaves of RIGHTEOUSNESS for holiness" (Rom. 6:19).

"For the Kingdom of God is not eating and drinking, but RIGHTEOUSNESS and peace and joy in the Holy Spirit (Rom. 14:17).

Whoever does not practice RIGHTEOUSNESS is NOT of God" (1 Jn. 3:10).

"Let us be glad and rejoice and give Him GLORY, for the marriage of the Lamb has come, and His wife has made herself ready." And to her it was granted to be arrayed in fine linen, clean and bright, for the fine linen is the RIGHTEOUS acts of the saints" (Rev 19:7-8 NKJV).

Righteous Judgement

"Let the heavens rejoice, and let the earth be glad; Let the sea roar, and all its fullness; Let the field be joyful, and all that is in it. Then all the trees of the woods will rejoice (clap their hands) before the LORD." WHY???

"For He is coming, for He is coming to judge (*shepat*, rule, govern, decide) the earth. He shall JUDGE (determine the measure) the world with RIGHTEOUSNESS (*tzedeq*), And the peoples with His truth" (Ps. 96:11-13).

God does everything according to His righteousness.

Heaven and earth rejoice because they are judged with righteousness.

NOTICE: THE JUDGEMENT OF THE WORLD IS TSEDEQ (righteousness in it's full meaning). Judgment is not about burning in hell fire forever, it is not legal judgement for punishment or retribution. It is the measuring the of rightwiseness and how we ruled in balance and maturity, being whole, straight, and prosperous.

Each thing rejoices because God's ways RIGHT LIVING, RIGHTWISENESS, bring health, bounty, true prosperity, and shalom.

Jesus LIVES IN YOU AS RIGHTEOUSNESS. You are found RIGHTEOUS at the time of any judgement.

"When the [uncompromisingly] righteousness are in authority, the people rejoice; but when the wicked man rules, the people groan and sigh" (Prv. 29:2, AMP).

"Indeed a King (*melch*) will reign according to righteousness (*tsedeq*), and the rulers will rule according to justice (*tsedeq*). Christ will reign through His helpers, the rulers, to judge people according to justice (*tsedeq*). The result will be peace!" (Is. 32:1).

"And I saw heaven opened, and behold a white horse; and he that sat upon him was called Faithful and True, and in righteousness he doth judge and make war (Rev. 19:11-18, KJV).

Let's repeat it: Material, emotional, and spiritual prosperity are part of the DIVINE inheritance of our mature Melchizedek rule.

SUMMARY:

Prosperity in every arena of life is part of your covenantal rights. Prosperity is your right ... God's *will is to bless you*!

TZEDEQ is your DOMINION RULE.

TZEDEQ is your apostolic governing platform.

TZEDEQ is your INFLUENCE.

TZEDEQ determines the *metron* or measure of your reach. It's the SCOPE of your ability to succeed. The Kingdom of God resides within us and grows according to the measure of the rule we have been given and that we inhabit.

YOUR TASK is ruling in righteous – Melchizedek king/priests rule the world in balance. Everything created in nature is subject to the governing prosperous rule of Melchizedek.

SECTION 8

King of Peace

Image KOP.org

Salem – Peace

Melchizedek was the King of Righteousness (*tzedek*) and Peace (*shalom*). He also rules as King within the jurisdiction of SALEM (Peace)

He is the KING OF PEACE, His ways are those of PEACE.

- Melchizedek was King of Salem (a place of PEACE)
- King of Peace (*shalom*, a condition or state of being)

We cannot fully cover the enormity of the phenomenal concept of peace here in this study. But what you need to know is that since the beginning, Jews have said 'SHALOM' in greeting each other 'hello' and also for 'good-bye.' Shalom means "peace to you." Basically, this Hebrew greeting means "be WHOLE and therefore you will be at peace." This wholeness is the integration of our spirit, soul, and body.[27]

 Every Jewish greeting and good-bye tells the other person to "Be Whole!"

27." (See 1 Thess. 5:23). Jesus often spoke about this WHOLENESS. He spoke to illness and said, "Your faith has made you WHOLE (sozo)." For details on wholeness, see author's book, "Connecting." See my book, *"Whole & Holy"* for complete teaching on body, soul, and spirit.

Peace Is the Emotion of Faith

Peace is that condition of heart that communicates to that the Lord is fully involved in the circumstances of our lives. Peace means that things exist wholly as God intends.

This Hebrew word *shalom* appears 250 times in the Old Testament. It is translated "peace" over 200 times. It has over 70 nuance meanings: Peace (07965) (*shalom* from *salam*/salem/shalam = to be safe and entire. it is the presence of WHOLENESS, completeness, sound, healthy, happy, perfect, complete, mature, well-being, harmony, health, welfare, safety, soundness, tranquility, prosperity, multi-colored, fullness, harmony, and rest. It is the absence of agitation or discord, a state of calm without anxiety or stress.

> Peace is a Fruit of the Spirit
>
> Jehovah Shalom is also a redemptive name for the Lord God.

Peace represents completeness, fullness, and soundness in your mind and physical body. Shalom also describes the relationships with God and His people. Several sources say that "Peace in the Jewish sense is the symphony of life made meaningful through a right relationship with God."

The similarity in the meanings of righteousness and peace is stunning. According to Strong's Complete Concordance of the Bible, *shalom* is the equivalent or close synonym for "prosperity" in a MATERIAL SENSE (cf. Ps 72:3; Isa. 54:13). [28]

Shalom, in other words, is "the way things should to be." It is the undisturbed freedom of life, the unchecked growth and expansion of those who are united together for the common good, the ultimate state all human beings and all things are able to be for fulfillment and without disturbance.

> David said, "There is no health (Ps 38:3KJV = "rest, harmony, wholeness" - *shalom*) in my bones because of my sin."

---

28. http://www.preceptaustin.org/shalom/definition

Psalm 76:1,2, "God is known in Judah; His name is great in Israel. And His tabernacle is in Salem; His dwelling place also is in Zion." Salem = is also Zion in the New Testament.

 Righteousness is IMPUTED and you can do nothing to get it: Peace is the essence that is IMPARTED.
Peace grows as we seek it.

That means you can FIND PEACE, apprehend it, get it, and apply it. Notice how your determined and focused EFFORT is involved:

- "Seek, inquire for, crave peace, and pursue (go after) it" (Ps. 34:14).

- Strive to live in peace. "Blessed are the peacemakers, for they will be called sons of God" (Matt. 5:9).

- "If it is possible, AS FAR AS IT DEPENDS ON YOU, live at peace with everyone" (Rom. 12:18).

- "Let us therefore make every effort to do what leads to peace and to mutual edification" (Rom 14:19, 1 Cor 1:10-11, Eph 4:3, 1 Pet. 3:11, Jms 3:17- 18).

Melchizedek King/Priests allow this progressive revelation to build in their "inner" being. They allow their trained senses rise up and take hold of this place of power. Perfecting peace comes through the self-government of the SOUL. The Holy Spirit is the Governor.

Shalom is God's gift (Isa. 66:12; Jer. 33:6) to provide wholeness, goodness, and complete satisfaction through the abundant life Jesus promised (Jn. 10:10)! Finding peace becomes one of the deepest longing and necessity of a believer's heart.

Peace, *shalom* is the undisturbed freedom of life and movement, the growth and expansion of those who are united in acting together for the common good state in which all human beings and all things are able to be and fulfill themselves unchecked and undisturbed.

Plus, the word *Salvation* (sozo) is a similar word to *shalom* and it also means "wholeness, rescue, safety, deliverance, forgiveness, protection, health, prosperity, preservation, freedom, liberty, peace, righteousness, and victory."

How does WHOLENESS happen? Here's the answer: The GOD OF THE PRINCE OF PEACE came to earth to present Himself so that we can find PEACE in Him!

It is the GOD of PEACE Who makes you completely holy - "May your entire spirit, soul and body be kept blameless for the coming of our Lord Jesus *(Yeshua, Yahshua)* the Messiah" (1 Thes. CJV).

It is the God of Peace who crushes Satan (Rom. 16:20).

We must learn this simple and amazing truth that Jesus (the Prince of Peace) said, "Peace I leave with you; my peace I GIVE YOU" (Jn. 14:27).

Peace is the doorway to revelation. His peace is His GIFT to us – it is a fruit of the Spirit (Gal. 5:22-23) that grows in us. Yet, we still have to "pursue peace" (Heb. 12:14).

King of Salem

Melchizedek was an actual king over a literal city called Salem (peace). Most scholars agree that "Salem" was the ancient name for Jerusalem. Of course, *salem* is the root word of "Jeru-salem." [29]

In ancient times, cities and people were named for specific reasons. "Salem" means a HABITATION OF PEACE.

Abraham LOOKED FOR THAT CITY (Heb. 11:10) – The great city of God. JERUSALEM is where God poured out his life-giving and power-enabling Spirit.

> This is the city where Jesus was crucified (Rev. 11:8).
>
> This is the blessed city that comes down from heaven – whose builder and maker is God. Zion – which also represents the Church.

Today, the actual city of Jerusalem is full of snipers, murder, bombs, and gripping conflicts. But, we are not looking for an earthly city! Our search is for heavenly Jerusalem, the heavenly city of peace.

Psalm 76:2 equates Salem with Zion, where the tabernacle of God dwells. The place of the tabernacle of God (Jerusalem) is located IN US! (YOUR (plural) body is the temple of the living God (1 Cor. 6:19-20).

> God's tabernacle is in Salem (Ps. 76:1-2). Salem (peace) is IN YOU because Peace is your reign. Melchizedek reigned over a place of PEACE where God himself dwells.
>
> Jesus died to enable us to live as WHOLE and HEALED people who demonstrate His Kingdom of PEACE *in this WORLD*.

---

29. Picture of Statue of Melchizedek. Santa Maria Maggiore, Rome.

The Vehicle of Melchizedek Wholeness

Many religions seek serenity – they desire an EXTERNAL calmness that is placid. But only the Holy Spirit can give us INTERNAL PEACE. The Holy Spirit is the Governor of your heart to bring your into full alignment with the Kingdom of Heaven here on earth.

Peace brings about controlled responses, emotions, and disciplines. This peace is tangible and, therefore, you can leave it behind (Jn. 14:27). People with peace can impart it to others.

> May (Jehovah Shalom, the God of Peace) Himself sanctify (purify, mentally consecrate) you completely; and may your WHOLE spirit, soul, and body be preserved blameless (every part through and through) at the coming (nearness) of our Lord Jesus Christ" (1 Thess. 5:23. NKJV).
>
> Each part of our three-fold nature (body, soul, and spirit) has the capability to receive or give impartation and new information.
>
> The accuracy of interpretation of revelation depends upon our WHOLENESS.
>
> WHOLENESS brings forth LIKENESS. LIKENESS brings us back to that FACE to FACE relationship.

We must rule over Peace as a KINGDOM in our heart (the Kingdom of HEAVEN is within). Only then, can it be released upon earth. When we come into partnership with God, we release heaven upon this earth. The heart of the trusting (without anxiety and worry) gives the Holy Spirit a place to REST IN PEACE.

 Pursing God's PEACE leads to WHOLENESS. Finding this peace is a great key to apprehending the supernatural.

Imagine this... Jesus was able to calm the storm by releasing PEACE, "Peace, be still" (Mat. 8:23-27).

Righteous and Peace Dwell Together

Melchizedek ruled over BOTH Righteousness and Peace at the same time.

> The Lord our Righteousness – Jehovah Tsidkenu.
>
> The Lord our Peace – Jehovah Shalom.

Trees of RIGHTEOUSNESS

Scripture could use any symbol for righteousness, but God chooses to use a TREE, "To appoint unto them that mourn in Zion, to give unto them beauty for ashes, the oil of joy for mourning, the garment of praise for the spirit of heaviness; that they might be called TREES OF RIGHTEOUSNESS, the planting of the LORD, that he might be glorified" (Is. 61:3).

> God is glorified because He plants the TREES of Righteousness.

"The fruit of the righteous is a tree of life" (Prv. 11:30). The FRUIT of RIGHTEOUSNESS (tzedeq) is a TREE OF LIFE – a continual source that keeps on providing sustenance, LIFE, strength, protection, healing, nourishing, and materials to build in endless supply.

When Righteousness is planted, it grows a TREE of LIFE.

> "And he shall be like a tree planted by the rivers of water, that bring forth his fruit in his season... and whatsoever he does shall PROSPER (literally, "to push forward and bring to perfection and wholeness" (Ps. 1:3).
>
> "They will be like a tree planted by the water that sends out its roots by the stream. It does not fear when heat comes; its leaves are always green. It... never fails to bear fruit" (Jer. 17:8).
>
> "And... the seed of the land or of the fruit of the tree, is the LORD's. It is holy to the LORD" (Lev. 27:30).

The Hebrew word for "tree" is *etz*. The first letter is *ayin*, is also the word for "eye." The second letter, *tzadeh*, is very similar to tzedek, meaning "righteous" or "righteous one." Perhaps the image of a "tree" was used because this Hebrew word could mean "the eye of the righteous."

The RIGHTEOUS inherit the earth! (Ps. 37:29)

PEACE is the Fruit of the Tree of Righteousness

A tree of the Lord is not just leaves – but fruit. Jesus cursed the fig tree that had nothing but leaves (Mat. 21:18-22, Mk. 11:12-14). The Husbandman is looking for the fruit!

Jesus said, "Herein is my Father glorified, that ye bear much fruit; so shall ye be my disciples" (John 15:8).

Fruit comes forth from the branch connected to the vine (Jn. 15:4).

The fruit is SEASONABLE (Ps. 1:3).

This fruit is INWARD fruit (Gal. 5:22) and also OUTWARD (Prov. 15:4).

Fruitfulness brings prosperity!

The Husbandman does not wait for our GIFTS, He WAITS FOR THE FRUIT of our lives (Jms. 5:7).

The tree is known by its fruit (Mat. 12:33).

"The root of the righteous yields fruit" (Prov. 12:12).

"Being filled with the FRUITS of RIGHTEOUSNESS which are by Jesus Christ, unto the glory and praise of God" (Phil. 1:11). 1).

"The fruit of that righteousness will be PEACE" (Is. 32:16)

PEACE is a fruit of the Spirit (Phil. 4:1-9). Peace is not a state of mind, or a circumstance in your life, it is a condition of your heart.

 Righteousness and Peace are inter-dependant.

Peace is a result (consequence) of righteousness.

James 3:17-18 also tells us that "The fruit of RIGHTEOUSNESS is sown in PEACE by those who make peace." The NIV says, "Peacemakers who sow in peace reap a harvest of righteousness."

The Fruit of Righteousness is planted in Peace.

Interdependence: SHALOM (peace) IS the FRUIT (produce) of RIGHTEOUSNESS (Is. 32:16). Righteousness is planted IN peace.

NOTICE the Scriptures that mention these two together: Please read these Scriptures again – now with new understanding

> "Behold, a king will reign RIGHTEOUSLY...until the Spirit is poured out upon us from on high... Then... the *WORK* (energy) OF RIGHTEOUSNESS will be PEACE, and the service of RIGHTEOUSNESS, quietness and confidence forever" (Isa. 32:1, 15).

> "No discipline seems pleasant at the time, but painful (sorrowful). Later on, however, it produces a HARVEST OF RIGHTEOUSNESS AND PEACE for those who have been trained by it" (Heb. 12:11, NIV).

> "Then justice will dwell in the wilderness, And RIGHTEOUSNESS remain in the fruitful field. THE WORK OF RIGHTEOUSNESS WILL BE PEACE, AND THE EFFECT OF RIGHTEOUSNESS, quietness and assurance forever" (Is. 32:15-17 NKJV).

> "There will be no end to the increase of His [the Messiah] government or of PEACE, on the throne of David and over His kingdom, to establish it and to uphold it with justice and RIGHTEOUSNESS from then on and forevermore. The zeal of the Lord will accomplish this" (Is. 9:7).

> Isa 48:18 "Oh, that you had heeded My commandments! Then your PEACE would have been like a river, And your RIGHTEOUSNESS like the waves of the sea."

Rom 14:17 "For the KINGDOM OF GOD is not eating and drinking, but RIGHTEOUSNESS and PEACE and joy in the Holy Spirit."

(See also Ps. 72:3; isa. 48:18, 60:17, 62:1; 2 Tim. 2:22; Jas. 3:8.)

They Kiss

"Mercy and truth have met together; RIGHTEOUSNESS and PEACE have KISSED. Truth shall spring out of the earth, And RIGHTEOUSNESS shall look down from heaven. Yes, the LORD will give what is good; And our land will yield its increase. RIGHTEOUSNESS will go before Him, And shall make His footsteps our pathway." (Ps. 85:10-13. NKJV).

The Messiah is both PEACE and RIGHTEOUSNESS (Jn. 14:26-27), which has been revealed in our hearts by the shedding of His blood.

When we rule over "righteousness and peace," we are that physical body or temple (1 Cor. 6:19-20). We abide in the heavenly state of mind. So when trouble comes (as it always does), our soul remains in the place (of kissing peace and righteousness) that our state of mind reflects.

SUMMARY: The Bible speaks of righteousness from beginning to end. Jesus literally took our sin in exchange for His righteousness. He has perfect standing with God the Father and now it is ours. PEACE is the fruit of having this kind of relationship with God.

Righteousness produces peace. And it is planted in peace.

Together, let us maintain the Peace of God that can only be mine through the righteousness of Christ. And that comes by understanding Melchizedek!

SECTION 9

Other Priests

Priests of the Tabernacle (illustration from the 1897 Bible Pictures by Charles Foster)

Other Priests

Within the scope of this study about Melchizedek are those Bible people who were priests with other designations. This following chapter attempts to explain the traditional Jewish views, history, and legends about the identity of Melchizedek. In looking at these ideas, please note that this is simply an "exploratory study." We are not saying it is Biblically correct and factual - other than being a fact that it was Jewish history. Hopefully, it will prompt you to ask some of the questions for yourself.

NOAH is identified as an ish-zaddik – or *RIGHTEOUS* Man (Gen. 6:9) and therefore, he walked with God. It was said that Noah did "all that the Lord commanded him to do" (7:1, 6:22). After the flood, the covenant was ratified and those who survived were known as the "RIGHTEOUS" people. Noah built an altar and gave sacrifice upon it as a priest (the first one). Jewish legend says that Noah passed this priesthood down his lineage.

EGYPT HAD PRIESTS: As mentioned earlier, there was a priesthood in Egypt and many priests who embraced their God Ra and many other national human deities.

When Joseph (a Jew) was exiled in Egypt, he was renamed "Zaphenath-Paneah" (thought to mean "My provision is God, the living one"). Second only to the Pharaoh, Joseph married Asenath, the daughter of a "priest" of On (Gen. 41:45).

Potipher (seems to be a title for the Pharaoh, rather than a proper name) demanded total obeyance and controlled all religion, all business, and all legalities.

"So Joseph established... a law concerning land in Egypt—still in force today—that a fifth of the produce belongs to Pharaoh. It was only the land of the priests that did not become Pharaoh's" (Is. 47:26).

MOSES: From history by both Josephus and Eusebius (chronicler to Constantine) Moses lived specifically during the reign of Amenhotep IV. According to the book of Exodus, Moses was born to a Hebrew mother, her name was Jochebed. Because the Pharaoh ordered all infant boys to be killed, Jochebed put him in a basket to float in the river where the women gathered everyday to bathe. He ended up being adopted by Pharaoh's daughter

Many believe that Moses was captured from the bulrush basket in the Nile and raised to be the brother of the Pharaoh Akhenaten. Their father was the Egyptian pharaoh, Amenhotep IV, and their Egyptian mother was Queen Nefertiti. When Moses returned to free the Israelites, there were many Egyptian priests.

JETHRO had seven daughters who drew water to fill the troughs to water their father's flock (Ex. 2:16). One of them married Moses. Jethro was called the "High Priest of Midian" and he was also called the prince of Median (Ex. 18:1). Interestingly, this is probably not the Egyptian priesthood. Midian Priests were believed to have existed before the Levitical priesthood was established. It appears possible that Jethro and the Midian priests may have been a part (extension) of the Melchizedek priesthood.

Medianites dwelt in Media (Western and Northern Iran).

Jethro was an Arab (Ex. 2:15-22). His name "Jethro" means "his abundance, or excellence."

By the way, "Median" was also the name of a son of Abraham and Keturah (Gen. 25:2). That means Jethro may have been a descendent of Abraham and could have learned about and even trained in the Melchizedek Priesthood in Jerusalem (see the chapter on "The Shem Connection").

There are lots of questions as to what a Medianite priest believed. Clearly, Jethro was not a heathen as he worshiped the LORD!

> "And Moses told his father in law all that the LORD had done unto Pharaoh... and [how] the LORD delivered them. And Jethro rejoiced for all the goodness which the LORD had done to Israel... And Jethro said, Blessed [be] the LORD, who hath delivered you... Now I know that the LORD [is] greater than all gods... And Jethro, Moses' father in law, took a burnt offering and (gave) sacrifices for God..." (Ex.18:8-12).

We know that Moses listened to his advice on how to govern the children of Israel.

Jethro was a priest of God BEFORE the establishing of the Levitical Priesthood in Exodus 28:1.

Magi (Plural of Latin magus; Greek magoi)

Darius the Great established the Magi over the state religion of Persia. It is thought that the ancient Magi of Matthew 2 were part of this hereditary priesthood of the Medes. The Magi were a group of priests who were attached to the MEDIAN court (See "Jethro").

The Magi were credited with profound and extraordinary knowledge. They also proved to be expert in the interpretation of dreams.

King Nebuchadnezzar appointed Daniel (a Jew) the chief ruler of all of Babylon and appointed him over these Magi priests. One of the titles given to Daniel was Rab-mag, the "Chief of the Magi." He was the principal administrator in two world empires – the Babylonian and the subsequent Persian Empire.

The Magi's court had great influence. Along with their religious functions (pouring libations into rivers and mountains, as well as making sacrifices of livestock), they were also engaged in administrative and economic decisions.

Living six centuries before the birth of Christ, Daniel certainly received and written down a large number of Messianic prophecies. Daniel was the one who received the Messianic vision that foretold that in due time a "star" would announce the coming Messianic kingdom (Daniel 2:44; Daniel 9:25).

> Plus the Angel Gabriel told Daniel how Jesus would present Himself as King to Jerusalem.

There is considerable Babylonian/Persian legacy that the "Magi" (of Matthew 2) were members of this same Median priesthood as Jethro.

Also being early astronomers, the Magi journeyed for about twelve months to go 1200 miles from Persia to Jerusalem. Their arrival to see the Christ Child (probably when He was about two years old) is the first time in the Scriptures where (other) people recognized Jesus as "Savior."

> No Father of the Church holds the Magi to have been kings, but rather good and holy men, who traveled from afar to seek for truth and to give an offering. (We think they were kings from the Christmas song.)
>
> The apocryphal Book of Seth writes much about the Magi legends.
>
> By the 6th century these three Magi were given names: Gaspar, Melchior, and Balthasar.
>
> The gifts of gold, frankincense, and myrrh speak prophetically of our Lord's offices of king, priest, and savior. Gold speaks of His kingship; frankincense was a spice used in the priestly duties; and myrrh was an embalming ointment anticipating His death.

Contrary to popular belief, the Magi were not originally followers of Zoroaster. That all came later. Their predecessors could have been followers of Melchizedek, and then after time their beliefs changed.

Beginning in the 4th century BC, the use of the term magi or magus became ambiguous and had a negative connotation. It often was used to designate conjurers, sorcerers, and soothsayers

ESTHER: Our chief source about the Magi during the Achaemenid period is the Histories by Herodotus who tells us that Xerxes (King during the time of Esther) did not undertake any important decisions without preliminary advice of the priests who were Magi. They interpreted his dreams and gave him prophecies; they also accompanied the Persian army on campaigns with the sacred fire (see, e.g., Hdt., 7.19, 37). [30]

Zadok - Tzadok The Keepers of the Covenant

After David's capture of Jerusalem, there was a sudden appearance of a group of priests called Zadokites. Some scholars believe that the Zadoks descended from the Melchizedek line and formed a sect that merged with the Aaronic line. [31] Zadok and Zedek are forms of the same root word.

Both names mean "RIGHTEOUSNESS." The Zadok priests were priests of righteousness.

Ezekiel portrays two categories or distinctions of Zadok priests: (1) those who were restored after falling away and (2) those who never fell away. While both groups continued as priests, those who had fallen away were limited in the priestly functions that they were allowed to perform.

> 1. "But the Levites who... went astray, who went astray from Me after their idols, shall bear the punishment for their iniquity. "Yet they shall be ministers in My sanctuary, having oversight at the gates of the house and ministering in the house; they shall slaughter the burnt offering and the sacrifice for the people, and they shall stand before them to minister to them" (Ezekiel 44:10-11 NASB).

> *"And they shall NOT COME NEAR TO ME TO SERVE AS A PRIEST TO ME, nor come near to any of My holy things, to the things that are most holy; but they will bear their shame and their abominations which they have committed. Yet I will appoint them TO KEEP CHARGE OF THE HOUSE, of all its service and of all that shall be done in it" (Ezekiel 44:13-14 NASB).*

Those who fell away were restored but could not come near to the Lord to minister. They could minister to the house, its services, and to the people. The second group, those who never fell away had a greater priestly function.

---

30. http://www.iranicaonline.org/articles/magi
31. Kaiser, Davids "Hard sayings of the Bible"

> 2. "But Levitical priests, the sons of Zadok, who kept charge of My sanctuary when the sons of Israel went astray from Me, SHALL COME NEAR TO ME TO MINISTER TO ME; and they shall stand before Me to offer Me the fat and the blood... They shall enter My sanctuary; they shall come near to My table to minister to Me and keep My charge (Ezekiel 44:15-16 NASB).
>
> In Ezekiel 40–48, these exiled Zadokites expected to be rewarded for their faithfulness and that the rest of the Levites would be reduced to the status of servants. The Book of Chronicles shows that after the return of the Jews, this distinction was discontinued.

DAVID: A *certain* Zadok Priest established a priestly dynasty from the time of King David to 171 BC. It is believed that this Zadok Priest was a Jebusite priest who lived when Jerusalem was conquered by David. He was in charge of the Ark at the time of Absolom's revolt (2 Sam. 15:24-37). After Absolom died, this Zadok (who was a seer) remained faithful to David and was made the high priest.

> I Chronicles 5:34–40 gives a list of the 12 generations of successors of Zadok.
>
> Zadok's origin is obscure. Some think that this man was the descendant of Eleazar, the son of Aaron. He is without reliable genealogy in the ancient texts.
>
> The Jebusites are described as worshippers of the same God (El Elyon) as the Israelites (and Melchizedek).
>
> A Zadok priest is also mentioned in the genealogy of Joseph, the father of Jesus (Matthew 1:14).

The Dead Sea Scrolls tell us that 'the sons of Zadok the Priests' had a central role within the community; they were called, 'Teacher of RIGHTEOUSNESS' (MOREH Zedek). They are also discussed in the Kabbalah.

> The Qumran Manuscripts contain extensive discussions where the "son of Zadok" is interchanged with "son of Zedek."
>
> The Qumran says that the righteous ones are "waiting" and "standing" to function at the end of days. It seems sure that Zadok and Melchizedek correspond in some significant ways.

When looking back at the history of the Zadok High Priests we find:

- The High Priest to King David and King Solomon was called Zadok.

- The first High Priest in The Temple of Solomon was Zadok.

- The last High Priest to serve in The Temple of Solomon was Jehozadak (Yahweh Zadok).

- The first High Priest in The Temple of Herod was Yahshua III from The House of Zadok (this may be the maternal grandfather of Jesus. See below).

- The High Priest at the time Jesus was born was Yahshua ben Sie or Yahshua V from The House of Zadok.

Jesus The Zadok

The Midrash Rabbah to Genesis, Tractate Nedarim, and Jewish commentators, such as Chaim ibn Attar, write that Melchizedek gave the priesthood to Abraham willingly. It is thought that this priesthood may have also continued into the Zadok Priesthood.

High Zadok Priest Yahshua III served in Second Temple; he had no sons but had three daughters. In order to maintain his Zadokite lineage, he arranged marriages for his daughters when they were very young (common at that time). These "daughters of Jerusalem" were in danger because Herod threatened them because he feared the High Priest and the coming Messiah. The three daughters were regarded as royalty. Their names were:

> ANNA (mother of Mary, also called Hannah) married the Maccabee prince, Alexander III Helios called Eli. Eli was the son of the Maccabee Queen Alexandra II (first known as "Esther of Jerusalem."). Anna was the mother of Mary.

> - In Luke 2:21-38, we read that Jesus was taken to the Temple to see the 84 year old prophet named Anna. Many Jewish legends say that this Anna is the grandmother of Jesus -- and she was hiding in the temple in disguise to be kept protective custody when He was consecrated. [32]

> ELIZABETH (mother of John the Baptist) married Zadok priest Zeckariah. Elizabeth was heiress of the Zadokite house. Her husband was the High Priest. Their son, John, was in the lineage line to become the next high priest.
>
> And the third daughter was JOANNA who was given in marriage to a Davidian Nasi and Prince of Israel, Joachim. She later traveled with Jesus.

When Mary became pregnant, she was put into the custody of Zeckariah and her aunt Elizabeth (who was pregnant with John the Baptist). By this time, Elizabeth was older and she and Mary were very close friends. Together Elizabeth and Zachariah guarded Mary to keep her child protected from Herod.

John was a Nazarite who took a vow to be separated, not to eat grapes (or liquors), not to cut his hair, not to touch corpses. The English word "Nazarene" (Greek "Nazaraios," Aramaic "Natsraya," or Hebrew "Notsri") comes from the Hebrew word *netser* meaning "BRANCH."

> In the Dead Sea Scrolls, "The Great Notsri (Nazarene)" and "Teacher of RIGHTEOUSNESS" had the proper understanding of the Torah to be the one through whom YHVH would reveal to the community "the hidden things in which Israel had gone astray."
>
> John the Baptist was often called, the "Great Notsri." He was next in line to be the "anointed High Priest" in direct succession because of his father and also through the lineage of his maternal grandfather, Yahshua III.
>
> That means, John the Baptist (The Great Nostri) was next in line to be High Priest and to prepare and reveal the coming of the Lord (Yehoshua HaNotzri – Jesus the Messiah).
>
> But, John knew he was not the Messiah. He escaped into the desert, protesting the corruption of the Temple and many Jews followed him.

---

32. Luke 2:36 tells us that Anna's father was "Phenol," which means "the face of God." From her widowhood, she never left the temple, but WAITED with fasting and praying night and day, expecting to see the promised Savior. And she did! Anna stayed in the right place until the right time! Luke 2:38 says "And coming in that instant!" Anna knew that He was worth the wait. When Anna saw Jesus she gave thanks to the Lord and "Spoke of Him to all those who looked for redemption in Jerusalem" (Lk. 2:38).

> Perhaps that is why Jesus said, (Matthew 11:11) "I tell you the truth, among those born of women, no one has arisen greater than John the Baptist."

Jesus could not go to the Temple for His consecration because that whole system was corrupted. That's why He went to His cousin, John, who was the legal next-in-line priest. (John The Baptist descended from the Levitical course of Abia.) John knew that his job was to "Prepare the way!"

Jesus was baptized when He turned 30 – the age of becoming a priest. It is believed by many Jews that when John baptized Jesus, he performed the ritual of *Mikveh* - that consecrates Jesus as The Levitical High Priest in this world! John gave Jesus the priesthood that he (John) had inherited by birth.

Jesus declared that His baptism was NECESSARY because it "FULFILLED ALL RIGHTEOUSNESS!" Be sure to let that statement sink in!

> At the beginning of His ministry, Jesus took upon Himself the Levitical Priesthood, the priesthood ON EARTH. He went into the desert and fasted and prayed.
>
> Jesus was assigned to bring the Levitical Priesthood to an end.
>
> At the end of His Ministry, after fulfilling all prophecy about Himself, He became the High Priest of HEAVEN, the Melchizedek of God.
>
> Here, we have the Melchizedek righteousness being fulfilled.

At this glorious baptism, John laid hands on Jesus and transferred all authority of his inherited Zadok Priesthood to Jesus. Then, John immersed Jesus in water making him ritually clean (sanctified) of all sin! (Yes. He was sinless, but as a human being learned obedience through the things He suffered. He needed to be baptized to fulfil Old Testament Scripture).

John said, "Behold! The Lamb who will take away the sin of the world!" It was here that Jesus became The Passover Lamb and the sins of the world had just been transferred on his shoulders by the next-in-line Levitical High Priest.

This transfer was in the manner that the High Priest laid hands on the "scapegoat" thereby transferring the sins of the people onto the spotless lamb on Passover and the goat on the Day of Atonement.

The resurrection of Jesus put an end to the necessity of annual sacrifice because He sacrificed Himself as the first born son of God. Once and for all. He satisfied the penalty of sin – death.

He became the Sacrifice and the Sacrificer.

At the same time that Jesus was given the earthly priesthood from John, the Father spoke the fullness of Who Jesus was in heaven, "This is My Beloved Son, in whom I am well pleased."

John	Jesus
Birth Prophesied in advance by an angel	
Father doubted Angel	Mother believed Angel
Miracle birth	Miraculous birth
His father was filled with the Spirit and prophesied	The Holy Spirit hovered over Mary
Had both mother's and father's bloodline was High Priest of Zadock	Mother's bloodline was priestly. His Father's lineage was Kingly
Parents were old.	Parents were young.
Elizabeth was barren	Mary was a virgin
Born to be Zakodite High Priest	Became Melchizedek Priest
John was the forerunner	Jesus was the Messiah (God)

Jesus is now the Priest and King on earth.

Jesus "went into the desert" – like the scapegoat of old carrying the sins of the world on His shoulders. He sought God for 40 days.

It was after this that Jesus emerged in POWER as the Savior and Messiah.

Jesus left that desert as the anointed High Priest and King of Israel by blood through His natural blood line! Now, you can look at this verse in Hebrews again, "Melchizedek" (as Jesus now was by inheritance or lineage a King of the House of David and High Priest of the House of Zadok). "Concerning him we have much to say, and it is hard to explain, since you have become dull of hearing" (Heb.5:7-8).

The writer of Hebrews said that Jesus was "unlike the other high priest" in the sense that he held a permanent priesthood because He conquered death and met the requirements of the Sacrifice.

It was the eternal plan of God to send His Son as the final Zadok Sacrifice to be the Passover Lamb and to become the Eternal Ruling Zadok.

At His baptism, Jesus became The Ruling Zadok on earth. At His resurrection, Jesus SAT DOWN in heaven. Here, He received *"ANOTHER"* priesthood that HE gives to us "INSTEAD!" Here is the END of the Levitical Priesthood.

Jesus became Melchizedek Priest at Ascension. "Now if He were on earth, He would not be a priest at all, since there are those who offer the gifts according to the Law..." (Heb. 8:4). In heaven, Jesus became THE Melchizedek, King and Priest of Endless LIFE in heaven and earth.

SECTION 10

The Keys to Heaven and Earth

"Christ Handing the Keys to St. Peter" by Pietro Perugino (1448–1523) Fresco

Bringing the Kingdom to Earth

My friend, don't be confused by all the other theories! What we know for sure is that TODAY you can live at this expanding moment on earth! The choice is yours.

Soon we find out that Lot is BACK IN SODOM! Two angels came to Lot to rescue him and his family. Lot "lingered" (Gen. 10:20) and the Lord was still merciful. "Escape for your life – run to the mountains and do not look back!" Lot ran to Zoar before the fire came on Sodom and Gomorrah. Lot's wife escaped and then turned and looked back toward the City and was immediately turned into a pillar of salt.

God allows you and me to make the choice – every day. Go forward or look back! Going forward releases the Melchizedek Authority in order to activate the energy (or power, *dunamis*) of God. That energy will expand His Kingdom on earth as it is in heaven! From **GLORY** to **GLORY**.

This CO-EXISTING environment is mobile. You can RULE in the Kingdom of God at the same time as your boss challenging you at work, your kids are screaming, and when you are racing to fill demanding schedules. Your Melchizedek co-existence is a convergence with God. Here are some of the ways that Jesus did it!

DIVINITY	HUMANITY
Son of God	Son of Man
Priest	King
Set aside HIs Godliness	Sacrifice for all
Lord of David	Son of David
Root	Offspring (Rev. 22;16)

Jesus is our First Fruit DEMONSTRATION! He came to earth in the earth suit of flesh and blood, as a human being. He walked on earth among us in a SPIRITUALLY-TEMPORAL SPACE in order to demonstrate Kingdom life that co-exists in both the spiritual and natural realms.

> He came as a man to show us that we can live the way He lived.
>
> He came as God to show us Who He is and how to reach Him.
>
> Jesus <u>NOW CO-EXISTS</u> on heaven and on earth.
>
> He gave us His Melchizedek priesthood so that we could have His authority!
>
> Melchizedek King Priests bring heaven to earth.

His New HEAVENS and a New EARTH "OVERLAP" into the space where we live. It CO-EXISTS with us. The Godly authority that we can exert on earth is directly proportional to the extent we abide in the heavenly places on earth (Eph. 1:20-23).

The principle of Melchizedek is that we can bring God's Kingdom tangibly to earth... Believers can co-exist with God (priest) while living and ruling here on earth (king) at the same time! We learn to live in the immediacy of the Spirit.

You are BOTH King and Priest

Right now, much of the church tries to divide the Body into two camps. They say that Priests are the ones who minister in the Church and Kings are those who minister and work in the market place or business arena.

As we saw how in the days of Moses a priesthood was formed through the lineage of Aaron, out of the tribe of Levi. And, another family line was set apart for being the kings, (the family of David).

- The king ruled the people and the land.

- The priest mediated between God and man through the sacrificial system.
- No king could be a priest, but he could be a prophet.
- No priest could be a king, but he could be a prophet.

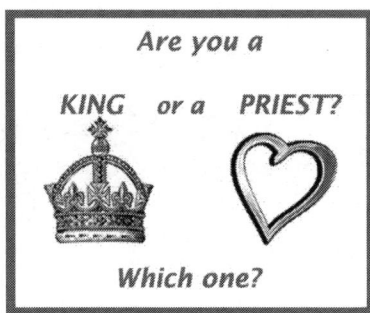

Of course, this separation causes lots of problems! As the Church redefines what we know for sure is that Melchizedek was BOTH a KING PRIEST at the SAME TIME!

One of the main purposes of this book is to show how Melchizedek sets the Biblical precedent that every believer is *BOTH* a KING and a PRIEST!

Let's assemble some of concepts that we have said before in different ways.

Melchizedek was a KING (Gen 14:18) who performed priestly functions. The New Testament does not teach that some people are "KINGS" and some are "PRIESTS," but rather, that we are BOTH.

Universal priesthood

1 Pet. 2:9
Rev. 5:9-10

- It is a *"royal* priesthood."
- The concept of NT Christians being priests and separate clerical cast from the laity is not in the New Testament.

Clerical caste   **Laity**

- The Scripture clearly teaches that individual believers are both KINGS and PRIESTS.
- While you may be more dominantly one or another, you can still fully function in both realms.

Ex. 19:5-6... *obey my voice and keep my covenant.... and you shall be unto me a* **kingdom of priests.**

GOD ALWAYS WANTED KING-PRIESTS!

In order for you to understand the purpose of your life on earth today, you must understand God's original purpose is for you to be a King and a Priest.

Every believer can fully function in business and ministry (bi-vocational). You are fully equipped to be able to be BOTH. This is the hour when the Lord ORDERS us to come into the full measure of our inheritance.

Kingdom assignments are spiritual... and natural. Whether they are about the church or about Kingdom entrepreneurial business, everything should reflect the will and purposes of God.

> King/Priests can use the Gifts of the Spirit to advance the Kingdom in every arena.
>
> Entrepreneurship is another way to support Kingdom assignments.

"And WHATEVER you do, whether by speech or action, do everything in the name of the Lord Jesus, giving thanks to God the Father through him" (Col. 3:17).

DOING BOTH

> Some tried to be both King and Priest – and failed. SAUL presumed to be both King and Priest (1 Sam. 13). That didn't work out too well!
>
> KING UZIAH burned incense in the temple (a function of priest) but 85 priests resisted his actions. Uziah was given leprosy and banished as a leper (2 Chron. 25).
>
> But, David did it! He became both! We'll talk about him soon.

You Are a King

You are specifically designed to exercise the intentional dominion (kingly rule) of creation and to manage the earth (your garden) and its resources. Just like that first human couple was commissioned to expand the garden in Eden to cover the earth (Gen. 1:28), this is the goal for all of us.

You have the kingly key! You are a KING born to execute, govern, control, and manage God's governmental rule over Righteousness and Peace here on this *EARTH*.

> God's will is to take place here on EARTH... "as in heaven, also upon *earth*" (Mat. 6:9, 10).

> "But the meek ones themselves will possess the *earth* and enjoy PEACE and PROSPERITY" (Ps. 37:11).

> As regarding this reigning, "The heavens belong to the Lord, but the *earth* he has given to the sons of men," (Ps. 115:16).

> The RIGHTEOUS will inherit the *earth* – And dwell in it *forever* (Ps. 37:29).

Jesus is the KING over all the earth and HE gives you kingly rights that flow from Him. The Scripture is your code of conduct, moral standards, and the constitution (Covenant) on how things are to be governed.

As God's ambassadors and representatives, KINGS establish the Kingdom on this earth and RULE on earth. Here's some of what kings do:

- God created a realm that needed to be ruled over.
- He created us to rule as kings over the earth in dominion.
- Kings have the authority to rule over all God's Kingdom.
- Kings extend God's heavenly government to this world.
- Kings have assigned sovereign territory (domain) over which God has given them total authority.

- Kings take care of others.
- Kings develop and establish the economic system that provides security for the citizens (seed time and harvest).
- Kings form armies to secure territory and keep it safe.
- Kings send ambassadors as envoys to represent him/her.

You Are a Priest.

> *"But you shall be named THE PRIESTS OF THE LORD, they shall call you the servants of our God. You shall eat the riches of the Gentiles, and in their glory you shall boast"* (Isa. 61:6, NKJ).

All believers receive a Royal Priesthood. Royal is the adjective defining the KIND of priesthood you hold. You are a Melchizedek king and a priest (1 Pet. 2:4-6). You are a "joint heir" (Rom. 8:17).

- Priests discern the heart of God.
- Priests receive the revelation of the Lord and His principles.
- Priests mediate God's purposes.
- Priests bless others.
- Priests discern, give vision, perceive, anticipate, communicate, and release heavenly realities into this tangible, natural world.
- There is no more daily ritual sacrifice for sin. His blood was the final sacrifice. You are only required to make one sacrifice – to present your BODY as a living sacrifice... which is your reasonable service (spiritual worship NIV, Rom. 12:1, 1 Pet. 2:9).

You Are Both

Both the KING and PRIEST offices function together simultaneously in the Person of Jesus. Zechariah tells us how the Messiah will be a PRIEST on His THRONE! Notice how this counsel of peace will be between the two offices; that is, both kingship and priesthood UNITED IN ONE PERSON (Zech. 6:9-15).

God is not just living on another far away place called heaven – He lives IN YOU. And it is THROUGH your priestly and kingly rule that His glory will be revealed to the world.

KING and a PRIEST

Augustine aptly said that *"Without God we cannot, without us God will not."* That's how God works with us. He won't do anything without the cooperation of His designated sons who are King-Priests.

Jesus literally rules through you as you apprehend your KING PRIEST position (see, Is. 9:6-7, Ps. 145:13, Dan. 7:21-22, Dan. 7:26-28, Matt. 25.34).

KING-PRIESTS establish His Kingdom on this EARTH

- While a Levitical priest could not own land or do any kind of business or work, being a Melchizedek KING-PRIEST allows you to have influence in all arenas.

- King Priests extend their influence into education, the arts, business, marketplace, and politics.

- You can be bi-vocational and actively a part of ministry at the same time.

- The Kingdom of God expands within you according to the metron of your assignment (the measure of rule you occupy).

This co-existing KING-PRIEST concept gives the Church the ability to effectively affect culture and impact the market place.

A King/Priest has the authority to restore WHOLENESS and healing in every arena of life:

A King/Priest lives in God's presence.

A King/Priest has both spiritual and governmental authority.

A King/Priest has authority over heaven and earth (what is loosed in heaven is loosed on earth, etc. Mat. 18:18).

A King/Priest has authority over angels.

A King/Priest has the authority of God to use His power over evil.

A King/Priest has authority to bless.

A King/Priest has dominion over this world and the world systems.

A King/Priest has the ability to transform cities and nations.

A King/Priest has the authority over sin and death. He/she bring LIFE.

A King/Priest leads the way overtaking the kingdoms of this world. "Then the seventh angel sounded: And there were loud voices in heaven, saying, "The kingdoms of this world have become the kingdoms of our Lord and of His Christ, and He shall reign forever and ever!" (Rev. 11:15).

ANGELS: The Levites had no authority over angels. But, Melchizedek King/priests have jurisdiction over the angelic ORDER, "Regarding the angels, he says, 'He (the Son of God) sends his angels like the winds, his servants like flames of fire" (Heb. 1:6-7).

One of my Ministry's slogans is, "The revealing of Christ in a people!" Jesus is (ongoingly) appearing and manifesting in YOU and ME as we take authority over existing systems. He who dwells within us is the hope of the glory that radiates *from* us.

It is the Father's good pleasure to GIVE US THE KINGDOM! (Lk. 12:32).

God planned for humanity to be His visible representative who would take over the *earth* (visible) and rule through the invisible (unseen) forces of *heaven* (Rom. 1:20, Col. 1:16, Heb. 11:3). He will not circumvent this plan. "The earth He has given to man." (Ps. 115:15-17).

The Great Kingdom of God fully came at the Resurrection - it is *already* established IN US (Lk. 17:21). The KINGDOM (place of rule) is no longer approaching, it is here!

- You are ALREADY brought into the Kingdom of the Son (Col. 1:12-13).

- You bring the Kingdom with you everywhere you go.

The more your mind-set agrees with His Kingdom plan, the more rule and access you gain. As the apostolic transformation of the mature corporate Christ arises, the ascension Gifts increase.

Melchizedek - Bilateral Co-existing

Most children are born Right-brained. But in Western Civilization, they are trained in school to be left brained. More men later become left brained than women. It seems possible that much of our ability to have spiritual insight was lessened because of overly left-brained acculturation.

That means that most of you who read this book are primarily re-programmed and now more dominantly left-brained-logical, intellectual, and objective thinkers. This left side naturally emphasizes performance and achievement. Of course, it is wonderful to have the use of the left brain, but you need both sides of your brain.

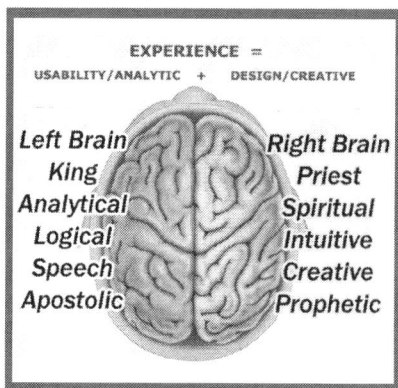

In most people, one side of the brain functions most of the time, but there are some people who can effectively switch from one side to the other very quickly. This of course is optimal use of the brain.

Our methodology must change, and our concepts expand. We can't continue to grind grain with oxen and wheel.

THE RIGHT SIDE (the more Priestly side): In its totality, the right side is a state of yielded awareness, alertness, composure, and physical/mental relaxation. Right-brained thinking allows for more creative problem solving because it is not saturated with logic and stress. It more easily taps into information stored in the subconscious memory.

Additionally (and importantly), the right brain controls spacial awareness, rhythm, imagination, daydreams, the perception of color, and perceiving alternate dimensions. It seems that the right side of our brain is more able to perceive underlying meanings and to creatively interpret greater applications.

The priestly mind-set can find God's will in heaven, but it can not transform society by itself - without the balance of the Kingly aspect that can advance that revelatory idea onto the earth.

THE LEFT SIDE (the more Kingly side): The logical left side is more organized and structured. It is easily bored and tends to "zone out" during creative right brained activities.

KING-PRIESTS See The Whole Picture!

Now we begin to renew our mind (Rom. 12) and transform our whole mind means you have PUT ON the NEW MAN and re-framed your mind for outrageous success!

Yes, even though you may have a decisively dominate brain side, you can learn to effectively use both sides of your brain! Melchizedek thinking exhibits the KING mentality coming together (co-existing) with the PRIEST mentality.

THE MELCHIZEDEK BRAIN:

LEFT	RIGHT
KING (Melk)	PRIEST (Zedek)
On Earth	As it is in Heaven
Natural	Spiritual
Soul	Spirit
More Left Brained	More Right Brained
Apostle	Prophet
The Son	The Bride
Earthly	Heavenly
Out-reach	In-reach
Establish the Kingdom	Serve & worship God

You are BOTH King and Priest

LEFT	RIGHT
KING (Melk)	PRIEST (Zedek)
Influence Culture	Mature the believer
External Change	Internal Change
Take the Trash Out!	Pillow Talk
Applying the Word	Learning the Word
Reason & Logic	Creative & Artistic
Orderly	Abstract
Compassionate Business Impact	Compassionate Evangelism
Action - Consequence	Worship & Freedom
Why & When	What
Transform Culture	Maturity, Wholeness
External Mission	Vision
Revolution & Occupation	Revival & Restoration
Strategy & Organization	Presence & Imagination
Ambassador	Evangelist
Enforcer	Inspiration
Procedural & orderly	Relational
Routine Oriented	Expressive
Focused on time	Not time focused
Earning Money	Spending Money

This study of brain side dominance is important because the two hemispheres SEE and interpret the world in vastly different ways. Inside each of us is "a war of the brain sides" where each side duels for pre-eminence - while the optimized thinking uses both sides and that is what is called being single-eyed.

The Revealing of Melchizedek

These brain sides already work together a lot. The right brain interacts with the natural realm as well. The LEFT side of our body is "wired" to the RIGHT side of our brain, and vice versa. This cross-over also applies even to our eyes; the right eye processes sensory data on the left side of the brain.

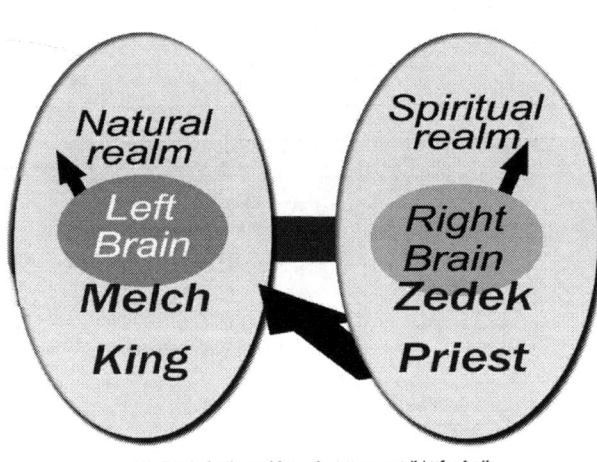

We live in both worlds and are responsible for both.

Optimizing both sides of your brain is how you become a KING-PRIEST! You can learn to embrace both sides of your brain. BOTH hemispheres are complimentary.

A narrow-mindedness (one-sided) may wrongly censor or prevent understanding.

You need to understand how to access each realm and know which side to use. Here's some more:

Left Brain - KING	Right Brain - PRIEST
Business	Desire & inspiration
Cognitive	Creative, inventive, intuitive
Linear thought	Intuitive thought
Details - trees	Big picture - forests
Looks at parts	Looks at whole
Logical	Spatial, random, imaginative
Analytical, concrete	Synthesizes to put together to make whole
Objective	Subjective, symbolic

You are BOTH King and Priest

Left Brain - KING	Right Brain - PRIEST
Facts rule	Philosophical insight
Math, digital	Spatial perception
Science	Beliefs & possibilities
Sequential order	Random
Pattern perception	Risk taking
Strategy	Music, art, gymnastics, & dancing
Practical analysis	Impetuous, unpredictable
Controls R. side of body	Controls L. side of body
One thing at a time	Multiple thought, sensory feelings, wholeness
Punctual, sense of time	Late, lived time
Unaware of surroundings	More aware of color & aroma
Strong language skills, rich vocabulary	Talkative, smaller vocabulary
Remembers words	Remembers smells, visual, sounds
Stress ignites process	Relaxation
Beta brain waves more active	Alpha brain waves more active
Temporal	Non temporal
Rational	Non rational, willing to suspend judgment
Organized, neat	More random
Truth, judgment, justice	Grace, life, liberty

The brain side that you use determines and defines your personality. The mature son learns to use both brain hemispheres in order to optimize and process valid impressions. Whoever you are, you can learn to incorporate more simultaneously left brained activity with right brained. [33]

Using Both Sides

KING – left	PRIEST - right
Kingdom	Church

The Greek definition of the Church (*ecclesia*) means those believers who are called out for revolution and reformation! They radically build a Kingdom with strategy and dominion (kingly rule). This demands co-operating abilities.

> As priests, we stand before God's throne.
>
> As royalty (kings), we exercise dominion over all opposition that seeks to rule this world. It is within us that these two assignments can harmoniously merge together.

EXAMPLE of USING SIDES TOGETHER: The right side of the brain would be more apt to discern the heart of God and (for example) WANT to feed the poor. The left brained function would strategize HOW to feed the poor – what steps are necessary?

The very first thing Jesus said in His first public address in a synagogue was to **PREACH THE GOSPEL TO THE POOR** (Lk. 4:18).

> *Preaching is a right brained function and the left side is social transformation. We need to have BOTH abilities.*

---

[33]. Please see my book "Connecting" for a lot more detail on this fascinating idea of brain dominance.

A King-Priest is open to progressive revelation that will modernize and reinvent ideas. If you are going to maximize your measure of influence and credibility it is vital to communicate spiritual matters in logical ways! He/she can inspire and minister to others spiritual concepts that will convert to strategic results!

HOW DO WE INCREASE THIS ABILITY? As Melchizedek leaders, we must develop an internal process for intentionally developing King-Priest leadership in others. We must ask:

- How can we mentor King-Priests?
- What Spiritual Gifts do they need? How can we help them develop those?
- How can we help them increase the skills and talents they possess to impact the world?
- What does significance look like? How can we move into significance beyond the scope of the local church?
- How can we know the heart-purposes of the Lord and translate that into a tactical framework of escalating success?

Keys

Jesus told Peter, "I will give you the KEYS to the KINGDOM OF HEAVEN." In order for Peter to understand this metaphor of a heavenly language, he needed to understand this statement within the context of ancient Scriptures.

It's really simple – a key symbolizes ACCESS – the power to open and shut! The ability to go in and out. Although in and of itself a key is not necessarily weighty or made to look important, it creates entrance and exit. A key is a physical implement that opens a door. A key can unlock a code. A key allows an entry into greater vistas on the other side. A key brings about change. The "key" represents the power to gain the heart of God and to the obtain the authority to rule on earth with the government of the kingdom.

Like we said at the beginning, the Scriptures are like a gigantic jigsaw puzzle with all the pieces available. Every piece must become a part of the overall picture. For centuries we have tried to understand how to fit this puzzle together – but what we haven't realized is that the picture to be assembled is a three-dimensional living concept!

At creation, the first couple were created in the image and likeness of God. They were given the specific task of guarding (*shamar,* meaning to observe, protect, keep watch) their Garden Paradise. But they failed to guard against the serpent. They hid from God and could no longer be a priest! A chain reaction was triggered.

Losing their King-Priest position caused the first couple to be banished from the Garden. The seraphim locked and sealed the Garden with a flaming sword (Gen. 3:24) that blocked the doorway to the Tree of LIfe and to Eden. The Tree of Life has **NO CURSE** on it. But, they did not possess the key needed to regain access to the Garden Paradise.

After the Fall, humans lost the KEY(s) to access the presence of God and to operate in His authority.

The **KEY** is the **REVELATION** of your identity of who you already are in **CHRIST**.

David had the Key

David, the unwanted shepherd boy, was overlooked by his family. While he was in the fields, he showed his fearless strength to kill a lion and a bear with his bare hands!

God sent Samuel to anoint the next king over Jeru-SALEM. David was not even invited to attend.

> Jesse replied. "But he's out in the fields watching the sheep and goats. 'Send for him at once,' Samuel said. 'We will not sit down to eat until he arrives.' So Jesse sent for him. He was dark and handsome, with beautiful eyes. And the Lord said, 'THIS IS THE ONE; ANOINT HIM'... Samuel took the flask of olive oil... and anointed David, and the Spirit of the Lord came powerfully upon David from that day on." (1 Sam. 16:10-12).

At an early age, David learned about unflinchingly facing his adversaries. Even though Goliath challenged Israel for 40 days, David faced the ominous Philistine with a sling shot and 5 smooth stones.

David was a King

It took David a long time to be convinced that he really was the king. In fact he was anointed three times. It was only after David perceived himself to be king (which he had legally been since a teenager), that 1 Chronicles says he obtained victory at Baal Perizim (14:11). One day it dawned on David that he already held the position and authority of that royal office. When he finally "perceived" it, then God was able to break through like water from a pent-up dam. Like David, all of us must perceive the fullness of our salvation, redemption, and inheritance through Christ.

 The KEY is *"metanoia"* – the perception beyond our understanding of just who God says we are – that frees us to love the world. Suddenly, from the inside out (like a volcano), comes the realization that son-ship made us the victor.

King David Knew How To Be A Priest!

King David participated in priestly functions as part of his royal duties.

David was born in the tribe of Judah and had lived under the Levitical priesthood all his life. Yet, he pressed into the things of God until it was said that he was, "a man after God's own heart" (Acts 13:22). His obsession brought him to the place of understanding how to be a King/Priest.

David took a small band of men and wiped out Jebusites and re-built this city to be like it had been under Shem's rule. David restored the old palace and once again, this city became center of government for all Israel.

> FF Bruce's Commentary on Hebrews explains that when King David conquered (Jeru)Salem and it was made his capital city (2 Sam. 5:5ff), "DAVID AND HIS HEIRS BECAME SUCCESSORS TO MELCHIZEDEK'S DOMAIN."

WORSHIP: Historians believe that many of the incredibly God seeking Psalms were written while David was a shepherd alone on the fields. Others were written at Ramah with the Prophet Samuel. David knew how to press into God.

Saul had a tormenting spirit that filled him with depression and fear. He sent for David to come play the harp. "He is also a fine-looking young man, and the Lord is with him" (1 Sam. 16:14-18).

- Because of David's understanding of Melchizedek, his worship brought the healing Presence of the Lord.
- Melchizedek worship is prophetic and solves governmental issues.
- Melchizedek worship rules over torment.
- Melchizedek king/priests have dominion (kingly rule) over evil.

King David knew how to function as a priest: When his men went to Ziklag, they found that city demolished and burned to the ground and his family was in great danger. Now here is the clue to success: "But David found strength in the LORD." Then he said to Abiathar the priest, "BRING ME THE EPHOD!"

Standing as a priest/king, David immediately encouraged and strengthened himself and prayed to ask God what to do about these raiders. "Shall I chase after them?" he asked. And the Lord said, "Yes, "Pursue, for you shall surely overtake them, and without fail recover all" (1 Sam. 30:1, 6-8 NKJ).

> "Go after them! Yes, you'll catch them! Yes, you'll make the rescue!" (MSG).
>
> As a king/priest David led war and won. (Levites could not go to war). This is the warfare of aggressively winning over principalities of cities.

His main passion was to return the arc. David (along with his men) brought up the ark with shouting and the sound of the trumpet! (2 Sam 6:14-17).

He danced before the LORD with all his might while wearing the *ephod* of a PRIEST. Michael, Saul's daughter, looked through a window and David leaping and whirling before the LORD; and she despised him in her heart (vs. 16).

It was forbidden for non-priests to do what David did. He wore the garments of the PRIEST and spoke blessings over his people.

 David's KEY accessed the heart of God (Acts. 13:22). As king, he danced in the streets with a linen ephod (priest) and ordered the ark to be positioned on the top of Zion. This KEY unlocked worship and unlocked God's Presence

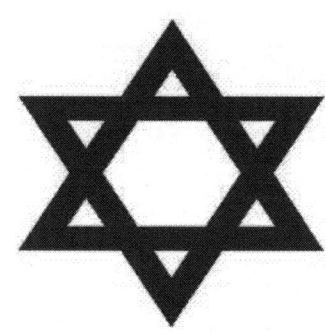

Somehow, out of the longing of his heart, David understood about a priesthood higher than the Aaronic that functioned in the tabernacle and the temples of his day. And the fact that David would know about Melchizedek is astounding. Here's the revelation of KING-PRIEST that we have studied so far:

    1) Creation order (The first couple were both king and priest)

    2) Melchizedek (King of Righteousness, Priest of the Most High)

    3) David (King and priest)

    4) Jesus and

    5) YOU!

At some point (probably between 1 Samuel 30 and 1 Chronicles 15), David discovered greater fullness about the Melchizedek priesthood: "My Lord' (Hebrew *ADONAI*) reigns as a priest forever after the order of Melchizedek" (Ps. 110:1,4). "Thou art a mediator, officiator with the highest charge of the ordination of the King priest of RIGHTEOUSNESS" (Zedek, Ps. 2).

How Did David Get This Revelation of the King/Priest and Melchizedek?

Uzzah was killed for putting his hand to the ark (1 Chron. 13:7-11). Why could David dance and celebrate with all his heart, but when the ark began to tip and Uzzah tried to protect it, he was struck dead.

The Scripture tells us an odd thing about this situation. When Uzzah touched the cart and died, David was ANGRY and named that place Perez-uzzah (meaning to burst out against Uzzah) (1 Chron. 13:11).

At that time, only the Levites were allowed to carry the ark. But, David believed that everyone should have access to God's presence – and so he was ANGRY! He wanted to touch God's presence and live!

David understood the priesthood of Melchizedek was a higher order than the Aaronic (Levitical) priesthood that was officiating in the temple at that time.

- No other king in history would wear linen EPHOD until JESUS came 1000 years later!
- We dress in fine linen – the righteous (*tzedek*) acts of the saints (Rev. 19:14).

David brought the ark (the container for the presence of God) into the streets of Jerusalem and then up to the top of mount of Zion (Mount Moriah). He removed the veil! While the Levites continued their empty ritualistic ceremonies, the ark was on the mountain in a simple tent, for everyone to see.

David was a KING and a PRIEST able to reach into the presence of God to hear spontaneous and prophetic Truth.

THRONE of DAVID: Jesus rules from the throne of David (Luke 1:32, Isa. 9:7). He shall build a house for My name, and I will establish the throne of his kingdom for ever (2 Sam. 7:1-29). "But I will settle him in My house and in My Kingdom forever, and his throne shall be established forever" (1 Chr. 17:11-14)

The Key of David – Eliakim

Isaiah tells us that God will place on Eliakim's SHOULDER the KEY to the house of David, what he opens no one can shut, and what he shuts no one can open (22:22).

- Eliakim ruled over the King's Household in Hezekiah's reign during the deliverance of Jeru-SALEM and Judah from the Assyrian oppressors.

- Eliakim's name (*yahki*) means, "SHALL SET UP" or "RESTORATION of the kingdom by Divine Power."

The "shoulder" represents the authority of both the King and the Priest.

- The "shoulder" is the symbol for government. Of the Prince of Peace, the Scripture says, "the government (KINGLY) shall be upon his shoulder" (Is. 9:6).

- The "shoulder" is also a priestly symbol of authority. The Levitical (PRIESTLY) breastplate was fastened upon the shoulders (Ex. 28:12).

David instated Eliakim as the chief steward. His official job was to reside "over the house of King David" when the King was absent. That means, Eliakim would rule in the royal office "in place of the king."

- This is a type of the rule that believers are given... ruling as a priest "in the place of God."

Importantly, Eliakim was called a *father* to the inhabitants of the kingdom. The KEY upon his shoulder represented delegate governmental oversight of the people and the needs of Jeru-SALEM, the Kingdom of David.

ELIAKIM HAD THE KEYS TO THE HOUSE OF DAVID. And these keys had binding authority in this administration. The decisions of the chief steward had the same delegated authority as that of the king.

Later, in about AD 97, the Apostle John wrote to the messenger in the Philadelphia (meaning brotherly love) Church, "He who has the KEY OF DAVID, He who opens and no one shuts, and shuts and no one opens" (Rev. 3:7).

Although this verse may fall powerless upon today's Church, the Philadelphia (brotherly love) saints had treasured up love for one another. What is important to see here is that the name "David" means "beloved" or lover. Philadelphia saints had the KEY of David because they loved one another.

Among the seven churches, Philadelphia received praise and not condemnation. They had "not denied God's Name." And, of the many promises given to them, they were to have the name of New Jeru-SALEM written on them.

- Jeru-SALEM is the place of rule for Melchizedek, David, and Jesus.

Jesus' new name would be written upon them so that the nature and character of Christ is imprinted upon and within their entire being.

Now notice this, although they were weak, Philadelphia had the "key of David" and before them was put an OPEN door that no one could shut (Rev. 3:8).

- Philadelphians understood this KEY. When someone in the Bible gives someone else a key...*THEY ARE IN CHARGE!*
- The Philadelphia Church knew the Scriptures about the Eliakim type government.

THIS DOOR IS ALWAYS OPEN!

An open door is continually in front of you – whether or not you chose to walk through the door is up to you.

What Was David's KEY?

 . David used this *same* key to RULE and conquer kingdoms. His governmental authority as KING unlocked dominion.

From creation to Revelation we hear a "loud voice from the throne" saying "NOW, the dwelling of God is WITH MEN, and He will LIVE WITH THEM." (Rev. 21:3).

 We see how David conquered cities and nations for the Kingdom. In I Chronicles 18 and in 2 Samuel 8 we find a summary of David's conquests. There is one phrase repeated four times: "The Lord gave David victory wherever he went."

David's KEY unlocked the revelation of being *both* a Melchizedek KING and a PRIEST.

- The salvation of all humankind is only on Christ's shoulders. He is the "door" that leads to our royal priesthood. Clearly, to this day, Jesus (a descendant of David) holds this Key of David and He sits on the throne of David.

Let's look again at what Jesus said to Peter, "I will give you the KEYS OF THE KINGDOM OF HEAVEN; whatever you bind on *earth* (natural realm) will be bound in *heaven* (heavenly realm), and whatever you loose on *earth* will be loosed in *heaven*." We see that repeating theme of heaven and earth.

- Heavenly keys lock and unlock earthly matters.
- Thy kingdom come on earth as it is in heaven.
- The Melchizedek blessing to Abraham was that he would be the possessor of both heaven and earth!

Right now, God looks for those upon whose shoulders (government) He can place the Key of David. You can receive and activate that Melchizedek KING-PRIEST blessing by faith – just like Abraham did (Heb. 11:8).

Like Eliakim, KING-PRIEST believers are delegated with the authority of God.

The Tabernacle Of David

Until this time, God's presence was reserved for the Levites, but at last, the KING PRIEST David made a way for everyone to have unrestricted access to the presence of God.

The Apostle James tells us that the TABERNACLE OF DAVID IS to be REBUILT (SET UP, restored) for a specific reason, *"That the rest of mankind may seek the Lord"* (Acts 15:16-17, Amos 9-12).

All of humanity will desire to seek the Lord when the tabernacle of David is rebuilt.

The Tabernacle of David represents the place where the two unique offices reserved for Jews by birth (priesthood was the Tribe of Levi, King was the Tribe of Judah) could be now held by everyone. This is a place for all people (men and women, old and young, every tribe and nation) to gather together.

Celebration was at the top of the mountain. Meanwhile, at the bottom of the hill, the Levites continued their empty ritual without the presence of the Lord. (Isn't that like a lot of churches these days, routine without presence!)

SUMMARY: Melchizedek was king of Salem (Jeru-salem), David was a Hebrew king who sat on Melchizedek's throne and ruled Jerusalem.

> One thousand years after Melchizedek, David had the KEY and he was "after God's own heart." He was the one who prophesied that Jesus would be the priest after the order of Melchizedek (Ps. 110:4).
>
> David built a altar to the Lord on Mt. Moriah on the threshing floor of Ornan the Jebusite (1 Chron 21:18). This was the same place where

Abraham offered Isaac (Gen 22:1,14), and where Jesus was Crucified.

Jerusalem (where Melchizedek was king) was the temple site (2 Chron 3:1). So we have a full circle.

The Melchizedek king/priest today understands prophetic worship.

TODAY

Church structure is not Levitical any more! No more liturgy. No ritual and routine. No sacrificial works. NO MORE trying to please an angry God! You and I are set into a NEW ORDER that can change our world. Melchizedek believers strategize to influence the world's cultural and society. They rise up spiritually to take dominion (kingly rule) through social action that fills the earth with God's glory (2 Thes. 2:1-12).

Do you see how the PUZZLE is fitted together as a living three-dimensional revelation of the unity of the Body?

The Corporate Son

The restoration of the tabernacle of God (1 Cor. 3:16)

The First Fruit Company

The New Creation (2 Cor. 5:17)

The One New Man (Eph. 3:15)

Children of God (Jn. 1:12

The Body of Christ (1 Cor. 12:27)

The Royal Priesthood (1 Peter 2:9)

The Bride

The New Jeru-SALEM from heaven!

We hear a new sound of shaking as God's breath enters us and our bones assemble together, bone to bone (EZK 37:4-8). The Spirit of God tells us to prophecy! Prophecy until we gather our bones together (Ez. 37:1-14) and stand to our feet as one exceeding great Body.

The *heaven and earth* join IN US. We become ONE flesh, bone of His bone and flesh of His flesh (Gen. 2:23). The Lord is assembling the King-Priest as His Body -- the temple (1 Cor. 3:16).

The Holy Spirit invites you to sit down on God's throne of abundant authority, and rule in victory. It's up to you! Will you? Become part of the new breed, hidden with Christ in God (Col. 3:1-11).

But, your freedom doesn't come all at once, it breaks through as you overcome the divisive OLD NATURE (feelings of confusion, hatred, prejudice, and offense) that has bedeviled and haunted your mind.

Now at last, you hear a rustling in the Mulberry trees – the turtledoves sing of reconciliation. Only then will your triumphant life bear witness to a lost humanity.

Jesus made it clear, "Destroy this temple (natural) and in THREE DAYS I will raise it up (Jn. 2:19-20). The Melchizedek believer will arise in the Third Day!

We become the spiritual Tabernacle prepared by Christ, dwelling in a spiritually-natural body that co-exists in *heaven on earth.* The seals are opening. The fullness of Jesus is FORMED in us (corporately) by the renewing of our mind by the Word of Truth.

- Cyrus king of Persia said, "The LORD, the God of heaven, has given me all the kingdoms of the earth and he has appointed me to build a temple for him at Jeru-SALEM" (12 Chron. 36:32, NIV).

- Ezra said, "We are the servants of the God of heaven and earth and we are REBUILDING the temple that was built many years ago...(Ez. 5:11).

Because we have the KEY, EVERY DOOR is OPEN! We don't need to look for open doors anymore!

Let us believe INTO Who Jesus is and embrace our destiny to set up this earthly Kingdom for eternal reign. YOU (pl. you and I) literally embody the TABERNACLE OF DAVID!

The rebuilding of the Tabernacle of David is not just about singing and dancing all the time – the rebuilding happens as each person envelopes their KING-PRIEST calling!

The KEY is understanding how to CO-EXIST as a *natural* person operating in the presence of God as a PRIEST – and at the same time, ruling as a *spiritual* KING in dominion on earth.

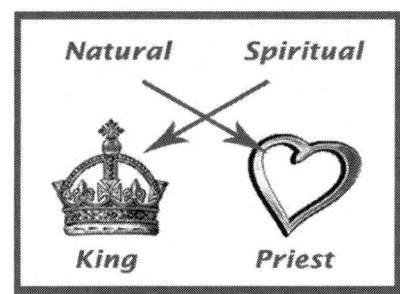

As KING PRIESTS step into this truth, we "Set up" the restoration of the TABERNACLE OF DAVID. This revealing of a new breed of people causes many to accept and believe the Gospel.

Jesus Is Our King-Priest

Two thousand years ago the birth of Jesus literally divided history in half. Now, the world measures time from His birth (B.C.) and after His death (A.D.). The life, death, and resurrection of Jesus was THE GREAT TURNING POINT – the tipping point – the FULLNESS of time, and the great divide of time.

Throughout the Old Testament we see the promise of this ruler King Who was to come. His mother's lineage was the line of priests. His father's lineage (Joseph) was the genealogical lineage of earthly KINGS.

He did not "honor Himself by *assuming* he could become High Priest... No, he was chosen by God" (Heb. 5:4-5). "He is the kind of high priest we need because He is holy, blameless, unstained by sin (Heb. 7:26). God elevated him to the place of highest honor... that every knee would bow (Phil. 2:9-11). God "qualified Him as a perfect High Priest and the SOURCE of eternal salvation" (Heb. 5:9).

Now this is the main point of the things we are saying: We have such a High Priest, who is SEATED at the right hand of the throne of the Majesty in the heavens, a Minister of the sanctuary and of the true tabernacle which the Lord erected, and not man" (Heb. Heb. 1:13, 8:1-2, NKJ).

- Jesus now sits down at God's right hand.

- The Levites always stood because their sacrifices for sin were never finished. Jesus sat down because His sacrifice was perfect and finished once and for all. He is seated. The sacrifice is over (Heb. 10:11-13).

- Christ holds all dominion. All things are in subjection under His feet (Heb. 2:8). Now, all things are under our feet because He ever lives IN US.

- In the midst of this changing world, He remains unchanged. As we move toward Him in revelation, our understanding changes of Who He is IN US.

- He brings many sons to glory (Heb. 2:10)! That's us. He calls us *brethren* (3:11).

- He finished what He came to do -- He does not have to come back and die again! It was the perfect sacrifice.

- The Feasts of the Lord, the Sabbaths, the Ceremonial Laws were all fulfilled at the Cross. They were temporal types of Who His IS (Col. 2:14-17, Gal. 4:10).

Old Covenant	At the Cross - NEW
The Law	Grace

Jesus gave us this "NEW ORDER" of Melchizedek and already MADE US KINGS AND PRIESTS unto God and His Father...(Rev. 1:5-6). He gives us a *better* **covenant and a** *better priesthood.* **As Melchizedek:**

He destroyed the power of death and the devil (2:14).

He gives sonship to the seed of Abraham (2:16).

He is the HIGH PRIEST who made propitiation for our sins (propitiation means that His sacrifice satisfied God, removed sin, and restored us to right relationships, 2:17).

He is the HIGH PREIST OF OUR CONFESSION (Heb. 3:1, 4:14). (Our confession builds our house (see Chapter 3).

We have a HIGH PRIEST who passed through the heavens (4:14).

We have a HIGH PRIEST who is without sin, therefore we can come boldly to obtain mercy and find grace (4:16).

We have a HIGH PRIEST who offered prayers and supplications to the Father (5:7).

We have a HIGH PRIEST Who obtained the promise (6:15) and this was confirmed with an oath (vs. 16).

We have a HIGH PRIEST Who is our forerunner having entered for us according to the ORDER OF MELCHIZEDEK (6:20).

We have a HIGH PRIEST Who is seated at the right hand of God in the heavens (8:1, 10:12). He ministers from the true tabernacle of the Lord.

We have a HIGH PRIEST Who obtained a more excellent ministry, He is the Mediator of a better covenant, with better promises (8:6-13).

We have a HIGH PRIEST Who, by His spotless blood offered once, brings us into the Holy of Holies (Chapter 9).

We have a HIGH PRIEST Who will appear a second time apart from sin for salvation (9:28).

We have a HIGH PRIEST Who is in heaven itself and NOW appears in the presence of God for us (9:24).

We have a HIGH PRIEST Who provided a NEW and LIVING way for us (10:20).

We have a HIGH PRIEST Who lives an Endless LIFE. He will never leave you or forsake you (13:5).

We have a HIGH PRIEST Who removed us from the mountain that burns with fire and blackness and into Mount Zion and to the city of the Living God, to the heavenly Jerusalem and to innumerable angels (12:18-24).

We have a HIGH PRIEST Who provides us with a Kingdom that cannot be shaken (12:28).

We have a HIGH PRIEST Who will NEVER leave you or forsake you (13:5).

"...That they may know more definitely and accurately and thoroughly that mystic secret of God, [which is] Christ (the Anointed One). In Him all the treasures of [divine] wisdom (comprehensive insight into the ways and purposes of God) and [all the riches of spiritual] knowledge and enlightenment are stored up and lie hidden" (Col 2:2-3, AMP).

It's not just about what Jesus did FOR us or what He gave TO us -- It is also about Who He is IN us.

We see our Messiah pours out to us a fullness of the Holy Spirit. He rules seamlessly today as the King of kings and as our Great High Priest. He presides over His creation as Christ, the Anointed One. He rules globally.

We are, as Moses, David, and the Apostle Peter understood, God's covenant people re-united and restored as a 'royal priesthood' and a 'holy nation'. (See Ex. 19:6 and 1 Pet.2:9).

Messiah is established as the RIGHTEOUS King on the throne of human hearts so that we can DO His work here bringing heaven to earth.

TWO BECOMING ONE:

The King and Priest merge as ONE.[34]

Both houses of Israel, the two olive trees, the two

---

34. This wonderful image of the dual olive tress and anointing is from the Jewish Cervera Bible. Spain circa 1299.

witnesses, and the two sticks of Ezekiel 37 become one, even a 'royal priesthood and a holy nation' (1Pet.2:9).

> The natural olive branches will be grafted back into the olive tree alongside the wild ones that were grafted in earlier.
>
> "And I will make them ONE NATION in the land upon the mountains of Israel; and one king shall be king to them all: and they shall be no more two nations, neither shall they be divided into two kingdoms any more at all" (ONE KINGDOM, Ez. 37).
>
> A man and a woman becoming One Flesh.
>
> Communion bread that is broken becoming one loaf and ONE BODY again within His Body as we re-member Him.

Of Jesus it is said, "...Yes, it is He who will build the temple of the LORD, and He who will bear the honor and sit and rule on His throne. THUS, HE WILL BE A PRIEST ON HIS THRONE, and the counsel of PEACE will be between the two offices." (Zec. 6:12-13)

Quickened & Endless Life

The Last Adam (Jesus) was made a *QUICKENING SPIRIT* (1 Cor. 15:45). The mystery of Melchizedek is enfolded within the mystery of the force of RESURRECTION LIFE. Jesus received His Priesthood after His resurrection.

This eternal LIFE is one of the chief signs of the Order of Melchizedek.

You are given the Right to Eat from the Tree of LIFE that was banished from the first couple. "...To him who overcomes, I will grant to eat of the Tree of Life which is in the Paradise of God" (Rev. 2:7).

In His ascension, Jesus opened the way for us to partake of His life-giving Spirit. We have access to Jesus, the long standing Tree of Life that resides in paradise.[35]

As we eat of this Tree, we partake of His flesh and blood – the ultimate sacrifice of Jesus and assimilate the priesthood that came from the Quickened LIFE OF GOD Himself.

"The SAME SPIRIT that raised Christ from the dead shall <u>QUICKEN</u> your mortal body!" This means now, in your lifetime you can find resurrection LIFE. You are QUICKENED FOREVER – meaning:

- To make alive. Revive - Make alive again. To LIVE. Resuscitate. To make alive; to vivify; to revive as from death. To live again.

- To be enlivened or communicate life. The action of Spirit upon spirit.

- Stimulate, invigorate, and incite - To sharpen, give keener perception.

- Kindle – to cause to burn more intensely

- To make more rapid: hasten, accelerate

- To come to life; *especially* to enter into a phase of active growth and development <seeds quicken*ing* in the soil

- To reach the stage of gestation at which fetal motion is felt

- To shine more brightly – watching the dawn quicken*ing* in the east.

- To become more rapid and accelerate- pulse quickened. Speed.

- Animate and gain action and character. To move with rapidity or activity.

- A sudden renewal of something inert – the arrival of spring *quickens* the earth

---

35. See chapters and notes on paradise and the Tree of Life in my book, "From Enmity to Equality."

- Animate emphasizes the imparting of motion or vitality to what is or might be dormant

- Lively - aroused from dullness or torpidity.

- Vivify to make alive or lively, implies a freshening or energizing through renewal of vitality (new blood needed to *vivify or give LIFE*)

- "You hath he quickened, who were dead in trespasses and sins" (Eph. 2).

- To cheer; to refresh with new revelation and increased Gifts of the Spirit (Ps. 119).

The Power of His Endless Life

Do you know the POWER of His resurrection? What does it mean? The obvious answer is that this is the *power* raised Him from the dead. Jesus had eternal life; death could not hold Him.

Jesus intended us to have a Melchizedek Priesthood – one charged with His power of eternal life. He comes to have you exchange realms and move into the LIFE of your perpetual Priesthood. The Melchizedek Order is the OUTFLOW OF the LIFE of CHRIST and the POWER (*dunamis*) of His INDISSOLUBLE LIFE (permanent, endless, for all eternity).

> "And *it is yet far more evident: for that after the similitude of Melchizedek there arises ANOTHER priest... after the power (dunamis - the power capable of reproducing itself) of an endless life (akalutos – not subject to destruction).*" (Heb. 7:15-16).

There is POWER in the Endless LIFE of Jesus our Melchizedek. Your heart may skip a beat when you fully realize that though you may fail again, fall, or slip into a downward spiral, He is able to re-establish our dismantled eternities, and set you within Him. He calls you today to experience a greater measure of His Eternal and Endless Life in the NOW!

This POWER is yours for the taking!

The word *dunamis* is the original of our word dynamic and dynamo, denoting a certain impetus, momentum, or causative force, which is cumulative, growing stronger and more impelling as it goes. It is a cumulative force as long as it continues. This word means continual growth and expansion of volume, filling you with power! Cherish this moment and open your eyes to the power you have been given.

> It is the unstoppable power to live your life with strength and vigor.
>
> It is the power to see afar off and project limitless possibilities.
>
> It is the power for advancement and improvement to build your life and to enlarge the Kingdom.
>
> It is the power to unlock the mysteries and discover the treasures of the unknown that must be made known – to bring heaven to earth.
>
> It is the LIFE-imparting power beyond the shadow of death.
>
> It is the strength-sustaining power of life abiding from the vine.
>
> It is the soul-satisfying Power. "He is able to save to the uttermost, seeing He ever lives" (Heb 7:25).
>
> It is the power of perfect blessing; the power of incomprehensible peace in this lifetime.
>
> It is the power to have clear prophetic insight on a city wide and national level.
>
> It is the power to have dominion (kingly rule) and strategic apostolic oversight.

Behind me is God's infinite power, within me is endless possibility, and before me is unlimited opportunity.

The angelic voices shouted in heaven, "The world has now become the Kingdom of our Lord and of His Christ, and He will reign *forever and ever*" (Rev. 11:15). This endless life is the "inheritance of the saints in light" (Col 1:12).

It is the POWER of the inviolable order of the world – a priesthood that arises out of the life that lives in Him. We partner within HIS priesthood and His manifesting power – and that priesthood of His ENDLESS LIFE is a manifestation of the Spirit given to every believer.

Other translations of this verse 16 give us a greater understanding of what that means.

- The Melchizedek King/The King/Priesthood is unchangeable, everlasting, eternal, and endless.
- Ours is a priesthood "by virtue of an indestructible Life (Wey).
- "... according to the energy of an indissoluble life" (Min).
- "But with the power of an imperishable life" (Con).
- "But on the basis of a power flowing from a life that cannot end" (Wms).
- "But by virtue of a life beyond the reach of death" (Tcnt).
- "Jesus made us a priest like Himself. He gives us HIS power – and that power is after His endless life."

That self same spirit that raised Christ, now quickens us, "…. That mortality might be swallowed up of LIFE. Now He that brought us FOR THIS SELFSAME THING is God…" (2 Cor. 5:1-5). You are I are destined for this selfsame thing! His Glorious Body (the Church) arises with the mighty working of THE INDWELLING POWER OF HIS RESURRECTION!

Continuing with Hebrews 16, "Who has come, not according to the law of a fleshly commandment, but according to the *power of an ENDLESS (indissoluble life,* perpetuity or eternal LIFE)!" ENDLESS LIFE! That's what He gives us!

His power was not derived from another man – it's not Levitical.

The power of this priesthood came from the LIFE OF GOD itself.

It's the resurrection power that arises out of the life that lives in Him.

Hebrews 7:17 tells us that Jesus was, "A priest for ever after the order of Melchizedek." He continues forever in His UNCHANGEABLE PRIESTHOOD (Heb. 7:23-24). Melchizedek "abides a priest continually." That Greek word "abides" is in the PRESENT tense, which indicates a continuous action of being a priest.

Jesus is held in the heavenlies until we "get this." Acts 3:20-21 AMP, "...Christ (the Anointed)... Whom heaven must receive [and retain] until the time for the COMPLETE RESTORATION of ALL that God spoke by the mouth of all His holy prophets for ages past (from the most ancient time in the memory of man)."

> That means, everything that was lost in the Fall and everything that was distorted by man's ideas and religion must be completely restored!
>
> Jesus came to seek and to save that which was lost (Lk. 19:10).
>
> The heavens HOLD until all is restored.

Yes! Jesus waits for us to regain the initial INTENTION of Creation! But think about this verse a little more... we can only gain this eternal priesthood through the SAME power that He gained it, that of resurrection life. He gives us LIFE NOW!

We are IN HIM... we need to meditate upon this truth. We are chosen in Him from BEFORE THE FOUNDATION OF THE WORLD, birthed again from above – into a new Divine family without genealogy! Death is now swallowed up into HIS VICTORY.

Our Great Melchizedek is ALIVE right now. "...of whom it is witnessed that HE LIVES" (Heb. 7:24). And, He "REMAINS (abides, a present tense word) a priest continually (perpetually)" (Heb. 7:3). We are IN HIM and IN His priesthood of Melchizedek.

Because He lives forever, we shall live also. "Wherefore He is able to save to the uttermost (limit of time) all who come unto God by Him seeing He EVER LIVETH to make intercession for them." He ever lives to pray for YOU!

The Melchizedek King/priest governs by a new LAW, that of the Spirit of LIFE (Rom. 1:1-2).

We rule over His priceless treasure, The Kingdom.

* * *

Many mysteries are answered the more you study the entire Bible and put the pieces together – and I pray that this has been one of those times. May you realize that YOU *already* are A ROYAL PRIESTHOOD releasing this same endless life.

Let us partake of the covenant by which all families on earth are blessed and receive the grace and victory of Jesus. And His name is RIGHTEOUSNESS and PEACE! These Names kiss within you. The bread and wine mingles INTO us with His precious endless LIFE. This is the riches of the glory of His inheritance IN THE SAINTS!

Let us ask the Holy Spirit to awaken these truths in our hearts—quickening them, allowing us to identify with the resurrection of Christ and understand our priesthood IN HIM.

The Beginning

CONTACT Dr. Kluane Spake

877-SPAKE-99   spake@mindspring.com

Mail: P.O. Box 941933 Atlanta, GA 31141

http://kluane.com

Leading Church Reform –

Equipping Today's Reformers!

DR. KLUANE SPAKE Is an internationally recognized and Commissioned Ambassadorial Apostle and Prophetic Keynote Speaker, Author, and Ministry Mentor to Christian Leaders.

This ministry exists to expand accurate CHURCH REFORM in order to fully activate the LIFE that Jesus died to give. To inspire, motivate, educate, and empower leaders with Present Truth Reform so that they can impact the Kingdom.

Dr. Kluane is a Theologian and Leadership Architect who continually researches to establish correct Biblical Truth and accurately translate eternal Principles into Spirit-Led practical application that impacts Leaders of the Church, Society, Governments, and Nations to change the world for Kingdom good. She is a friend to the Body of Christ.

We help passionate Christian Leaders and Ministers succeed! Our mandate is to release: The "Revealing of Christ in a People" and that includes teaching Present Truth, Life-changing Third Day Reformational concepts, The Direction of the Future Church, Apostolic Government, and the fullness of the Finished Work of Redemption to the nations.

For Leadership empowerment, she established "The School of the Apostles." Online Bible School, and has written over 25 Books and countless E-books and articles. And lots more courses are coming soon!

Dr. Kluane was raised in Alaska and later moved to Guam for 15 years. She now lives in Atlanta area with her husband and family.
spake@mindspring.com   http://kluane.com   218-248-7247 -

Bibliography

Copyright applied in 2014 by Dr. Kluane Spake, http://kluane.com &.org

The author does not give the right to redistribute without prior consent and in writing of the information herein. All rights of this book are reserved worldwide. No portion of this book may be transmitted or copied in any form or by any means – electronic, mechanical, photocopy, recording, or any other without author's permission.

I believe this manuscript conforms to Copyright laws in America and would be grateful if any unintentional lapses would be drawn to my attention. Scriptures may be personalized, paraphrased, abridged, expanded, or conformed to the person and tense of the contextual application to foster clarity and to broaden individual application. Various languages and versions have been sometimes combined. The reader is encouraged to compare these passages with his or her own Bible. Some of the ideas herein may be from copious notes from tapes, seminars, and internet articles collected over the years – unfortunately, not knowing some sources. Also, this book contains many of the ideas and words of authors listed in bibliography and others.

Selected information from these sources may be paraphrased, summarized, or used with their verbatim apt phrases, sections, and ideas. I am grateful for their research. My apologies for any inadvertent lack of documentation. Some HISTORICAL references are not necessarily Christian sources. Some of this book comes from my book, "Connecting." Some of it is taken from excerpts from my DVD Melchizedek Reality and my internet articles. Pictures are mostly mine and some Google images that did not have references or names.

spake, kluane, dvd series melchizedek reality

spake, kluane, Connecting, Apprehending Spiritual Realities

spake, kluane, wisdom

http://www.betemunah.org/priests.html

http://www.bible.ca/d-15-antitypes-gen14-15-abram-melchizedek-lot.htm

http://bibletimeline.net/biblehistoryblog/biblical-timeline-son-of-noah

http://bibleconundrumsandcontroversy.blogspot.com/2011/01.html

http://www.centralbaptistchurch.org/wp-content/uploads/2010/11/Genesis-14.pdf

http://www.donmeh-west.com - Oral Torah

http://drkluanespake.hubpages.com/hub/Christian-Our-Priesthood-of-Prosertiy

http://drkluanespake.hubpages.com/hub/Who-was-Melchizedek

http://faithtalkministries.com/blog-2/ image, tree.

http://www.hebrew4christians.com/Scripture/Parashah/Lekh_Lekha/Melchizedek/

http://kgov.com/caanan

http://www.ldolphin.org/magi.html

www.lifestreamteaching.com

http://www.sigler.org/eby/priest24.html endless

http://www.freerepublic.com/focus/f-religion/3027522/posts

http://israelofgod.org/htm

https://www.jewishvirtuallibrary.org/jsource/judaica/ejud_html

http://www.kingshouse.org/priests.htm

http://leisure.article-presser.com/facts-about-ancient-jerusalem

http://www.letusreason.org/Doct16.htm

http://members.efn.org/~opal/therealmagi.html

http://www.sabbathcovenant.com/Book%204_Melchizedek/chapter1-4

http://readthebiblewithme.wordpress.com/2013/07/26/genesis-14

http://theonlinebibleschool.net/mod/resource/view.php

http://www.pbc.org/files/messages/6813/3885.html

http://roberteisenman.com/articles/zaddik_idea Zadok

http://www.sabbathcovenant.com/Book%204_Melchizedek/chapter1-4

http://www.scribd.com/doc/3913

http://ulrikegrace.hubpages.com/hub/The-Melchizedek

http://en.wikipedia.org/wiki/ Several topics.

plus hundreds of other source!

* * *

Clarke, Adam. <u>Clarkes Commentary</u>. Abingdon Press: New York. Vol. 3.

Conner, Kevin, "The Lord Jesus Christ Our Melchizedek" City Life Distributors, Victoria, AU 2008

M'Clintock, John and James Strong. <u>Cyclopedia of Biblical, Theological, and Ecclesiastical Literature</u>. Baker Book House: Grand Rapids. Vol. 6. Reprinted in 1969.

Myles, Frances, "The Order of Melchizedek" Word and Spirit Books, Tulsa, OK, 74170, 1 Pet. 2:4-6, Lachan, David, and two seed lines of Abram.

ENDNOTES:

Spence, H. D. M. and Joseph S. Exell. <u>The Pulpit Commentary</u>. WM. B. Eerdman's Publishing Company. Reprinted in 1962.

Segraves, Daniel L. <u>Hebrews: Better Things</u>. Vol. 1. Hazelwood, MO: Word Aflame Press. 1996.

Stone, Michael & Bergren, Theodore, <u>Biblical Figures Outside the Bible</u>, Trinity Press, 1998

Stine, W. E., Merril F. Unger, William White, Jr. <u>Vine's Complete Expository Dictionary of Old and New Testament Words</u>. Nashville: Thomas Nelson Publishers, 1984.

Clarke, Adam, LL.D., F.S.A., &c. <u>Clark's Commentary</u>, vol. 6. Nashville, TN. Abingdon Press.

Wood, Paul, "third level tithing, www.xulonpress.com

Tuck, Robert, B. A. (Lond.) <u>A Homiletic Commentary on the Epistle to the Hebrews</u>. New York and London. Funk & Wagnalls Company.

Pentecost, J. Dwight <u>Things to Come</u>. Grand Rapids, MI. Zondervan Pub. House, 1958.

Turner, Nigel <u>A Grammar of New Testament Greek</u>. 38 George Street, Edinburgh. T. & T. Clark, 1963.

ENDNOTES:

THE DEVIL

The devil was delivered into the hands of Jesus and no longer has the hold of spiritual death over humanity. Paul emphasized this when he said, "Forasmuch then as the children are partakers of flesh and blood, he [the Messiah] also himself likewise took part of the same; THAT THROUGH DEATH HE MIGHT DESTROY HIM THAT HAD THE POWER OF DEATH, THAT IS, THE DEVIL; And deliver them who through fear of death were all their lifetime subject to bondage. For verily he took not on him the nature of angels; but he took on him the seed of Abraham. Wherefore in all things it behoved him to be made like unto his brethren, that he might be a merciful and faithful high priest in things pertaining to Elohim (God), to make reconciliation for the sins of the people" (Heb. 2:14-17).

HASHEM

HaShem is the Hebrew word which most Jews use instead of the yod-hey-vav-hey (הוהי–YHVH[1]) name, in casual conversations. HaShem literally means "The Name." (Same as the meaning of Shem.) Jews encounter this name during prayers or when reading from the Torah, they visualize הוהי and say Adonai. HaShem is used 7484 times in the Tanach[2]. Neither HaShem, nor it's Greek equivalent is ever used in the Nazarean Codicil.[4] The first use, of HaShem, is in the Bereshit.

Bereshit (Genesis) 2:4 This is the account of the heavens and the earth when they were created. When HaShem God made the earth and the heavens--

In the NIV, KJV, and the Jerusalem Bibles they use "LORD" instead of HaShem. The NASB uses "Lord" instead of HaShem. Bereshit (Genesis) 2:4 This is the account of the heavens and the earth when they were created. When *HaShem* God made the earth and the heavens--

Bereshit (Genesis) 12:6-9 And Abram passed through the land unto the place of Sichem, unto the plain of Moreh. And the Canaanite [was] then in the land. And the HaShem appeared unto Abram, and said, Unto thy seed will I give this land: and there built he an altar unto the HaShem, who appeared unto him. And he removed from thence unto a mountain on the east of Beth-el, and pitched his tent, [having] Beth-el on the west, and Hai on the east: and there he built an altar unto the HaShem, and called upon the name of the HaShem. And Abram journeyed, going on still toward the south.

Bereshit (Genesis) 13:1-4 So Abram went up from Egypt to the Negev... until he came to the place between Bethel and Ai where his tent had been earlier And where he had first built an altar. There Abram called on the name of HaShem.

Bereshit (Genesis) 13:2-4 And Abram [was] very rich in cattle, in silver, and in gold. And he went on his journeys from the south even to Beth-el, unto the place where his tent had been at the beginning, between Beth-el and Hai; Unto the place of the altar, which he had made there at the first: and there Abram called on the name of HaShem.

Bereshit (Genesis) 21:33 And [Abraham] planted a grove in Beer-sheba, and called there on the name of HaShem, the everlasting God.[36]

THE MELCHIZEDEK TEACHINGS IN THE OCCIDENT

1. THE SALEM RELIGION AMONG THE GREEKS

The basic doctrines of Greek philosophy were fundamentally repercussions of the earlier Melchizedek teachings. Salem missionaries sustained ritual groups.

The practice of observing Melchizedek tradition and monotheism began early. Melchizedek teachers penetrated to pre-Hellenic Greece. The Aryan invasion nearly destroyed these people and brought with it the ideas of Greek gods and goddesses, cults, and the myths of the older inhabitants of Greece.

Hellenic Greeks imposed their conception of subordinate gods. Zeus became the final controller of their fate. But the average Greeks could not understand this complex Greek philosophy of self-realization.

2, IN ROME

There was also a strong Etruscan priesthood with its new galaxy of gods and temples, which became the Roman state religion. there was also a great monotheistic renaissance of Melchizedek's Salem groups during the sixth century before Christ.

Roman religion later became greatly influenced by Greeks. Eventually the names of most of their Olympian gods were changed and incorporated into the Latin. The Greeks worshiped Hestia, the virgin goddess of the hearth; and the Romans worshiped the counterpart, Vesta,

---

36.http://www.betemunah.org/hashem.html

ENDNOTES:

the goddess of the home; Zeus became Jupiter; Aphrodite became Venus, etc. The greatest cult was the mystery religion of the Mother of Goddess which once headquartered on the exact site of the present church of St. Peter's in Rome.

SECRET IDEAS: From both Greece and Rome, several Melchizedek legends,

Stories, cultish ideas, and secret societies arose... and there were even some who believe that Melchizedek descended from an alien race from another planet in a far away galaxy.

Here are just a few records regarding Melchizedek. By mentioned these historic documents, we in no way give credence to their validity - merely documenting what has been said outside the Scriptures.

The Pseudepigrapha fragments mention Gamaliel who wrote, *"But all the tribes and all the peoples will speak the truth who are receiving from you yourself, O Melchizedek, Holy One, High-Priest, the perfect hope and the gifts of life. I am Gamaliel, who was sent to [...] the congregation of the children of Seth, who are above thousands of thousands, and myriads of myriads, of the aeons [...] of the aeons, aba[...]!"*

In the Second Book of Jeu, "Zorokothora Melchizedek" is a heavenly priest who presides over a heavenly baptism. No trace of influence from Hebrews is found in this text.

Jewish speculation on Melchizedek has surfaced among fragments of the Dead Sea Scrolls (11QMelch). These seemingly Gnostic Hebrew text, dated to the first century B.C., speak of Melchizedek as the creator and the heavenly end-time redeemer.

In the Dead Sea Scrolls 11QMelchizedek (11Q13), a sectarian text in which Melchizedek is understood to be an angel probably identical to the archangel Michael and the Prince of Light that are discussed in other Qumran sectarian writings.

PHILO, a first-century Jewish philosopher of Alexandria, talks about Melchizedek in three writings. [37] He writes, *"Melchizedek also has God made both king of peace, for that is the meaning of Salem, and his own priest...a king peaceable and worthy of his [God's] own priesthood. For he is entitled 'the righteous king', and a king is at enmity with a despot, the one being the author of laws, the other of lawlessness"* (Leg. All. 3. 25-26 33 79-82).

JOSEPHUS explains: *Abram "was received by the king of Solyma [Salem], Melchizedek; the name means 'righteous king', and such he was by common consent, inasmuch for this reason he was moreover made priest of God; Solyma was in fact the place afterward called Hierosolyma [Jerusalem]"* (Ant. 1.10.2).

THE APROCHRYPAL BOOK OF ENOCH

The text states Methusaleh (translated as Methusalem) had a child named Lamech, and his son was named Nir. Nir is identified in this text as the father of Melchizedek.

2 Enoch tells about (chaps. 71-72), a child who is born miraculously to Noah's sister-in-law, who died at birth. This boy is supposedly already 3 years old when delivered. Noah and his brother Nir named the child Melchizedek. Having been warned of the impending flood, Nir instructed the archangel Michael to take Melchizedek to paradise to escape the flood waters.

---

37. Legum Allegoriae 3.79-82; De Congressu 89; De Abraham 235

Melchizedek was to eventually become the chief of priests, and in later reference, another Melchizedek that would come later.[38] A fragmentary text from Nag Hammadi[39] contains an apocalypse given by angels to Melchizedek stating that he will ultimately reappear as Jesus Christ to battle with darkness.

Books 1-3 of Pistis Sophia develops these ideas further: Melchizedek is a heavenly being who seals the saved souls upon their entry into the realm of light.

ABD-KHIBA At least six letters written in 1450 BC were discovered in the Tell el-Amarna Letters from Abd-Khiba who was king of Urisalim -- written to Amenophis IV, King of Egypt. *Urusalim* is assumed to be an ancient name for Jerusalem -- and, if so, this is the earliest mention of that city. **A**bd-Khiba writes, "Neither my father nor my mother set me in this place: the mighty arm of the king established me in my father's house."[40]

Some tradition identifies Melchizedek as being this same Abd-Khiba. The idea that he had not "genealogy" was because he acknowledged that he did not become ruler through descent; but that he was appointed by Amenophis IV.

NOAH: An ancient Jewish cult of cabalistic tradition taught that Melchizedek's secret identity is Noah, who taught humanity agriculture, and who (according to their story) never really died but transitioned into another dimension so that he could reappeared as Abraham's spiritual teacher and to initiate him to a higher level.

This is an excerpt from the Book of Melchizedek: *'My father commanded me to go and see the sources of the rivers and the seas and the structure of the earth, and to return.' And he said to Mâlâh the father of Melchizedek, and to Yôzâdâk his mother, 'Give me your son that he may be with me, and behold, my wife and my children are with you.' Melchizedek's parents said to him, 'My lord, take thy servant; and may the angel of peace be with thee...' Shem went by night into the ark, and took Adam's coffin; and he sealed up the ark... And he journeyed by night with the angel ... and Melchizedek with him, until they came and stood upon the spot where our Lord was crucified.*

When they had laid the coffin down there, the earth was rent in the form of a cross1, and swallowed up the coffin, and was again sealed up and returned to its former condition. Shem laid his hand upon Melchizedek's head, and blessed him, and delivered to him the priesthood, and commanded him to dwell there until the end of his life...

And Shem returned to... Melchizedek's parents (and) said to him, 'Where is our son?' Shem said, 'He died while he was with me on the way, and I buried him;' and they mourned for him a month of days; but Melchizedek dwelt in that place until he died.

When he was old, the kings of the earth heard his fame, and eleven of them gathered together and came to see him;... he would not be persuaded... They built a city for him there, and he called it Jerusalem... When Abraham came back from the battle of the kings and the nations, he passed by the mount of Jerusalem; and Melchizedek came forth to meet him, and

---

38. The Book of the Secrets of Enoch translated by W.R. Morfill and R.H. Charles (Oxford Clarendon Press, Oxford, England, 1896), Appendix, pgs 88-92
39. IX.1: Melchizedek; cf. Pearson, 1981,pp. 19-85
40. Tell el-Amarna Letters, Letter 102 in Berlin collection, ll. 9-13; also number 103, ll. 25-28; number 104, ll. 13-15; International Standard Bible Encyclopaedia

ENDNOTES:

Abraham made obeisance to Melchizedek, and gave him tithes of all that he had with him. And Melchizedek embraced him and blessed him, and gave him bread and wine...

MEDIA, MAJI: Josephus relates the Medes (OT Heb. Madai) to the biblical character, Madai, son of Japheth. "Now as to Javan and Madai, the sons of Japhet; from Madai came the Madeans, who are called Medes, by the Greeks" Antiquities of the Jews, I:6.

In the Aggadah, Jethro was a priest from Egypt. His name is sometimes thought to also be Ruelel.

PRIESTS: In Genesis 41:45,50; 46:20 we also see another kind of priest "...Potipherah priest of On. Potipherah means "he whom the Ra gave." Ra was the Egyptian pagan so-called god of the Sun.

LIFE Romans 8:4 in order that the *RIGHTOUS requirement of the law* might be *fully met* in us (we would be restored to perfection), who do not live according to the flesh (which is hostile to The Law) but according to the Spirit (whose mind is set on The Law as we obey it in love not obligation). 6 The mind governed by the flesh is death (the penalty levied for transgressing), but the mind governed by the Spirit is life and peace (the promise).

THE COMING OF MELCHIZEDEK, Dead Sea Scroll: 11Q13, Column 2 as follows to end.

Deut.15;2 just as Isaiah said: To proclaim the Jubilee to the captives" (Isa. 61;1) (...) just as (...) and from the inheritance of Melchizedek, for (... Melchizedek), who will return them to what is rightfully theirs. He will proclaim to them the Jubilee, thereby releasing them from the debt of all their sins. He shall proclaim this decree in the first week of the jubilee period that follows nine jubilee periods. Then the "Day of Atonement" shall follow after the tenth jubilee period, when he shall atone for all the Sons of Light, and the people who are predestined to Melchizedek. (...) upon them (...) For this is the time decreed for the "Year of Melchizedek`s favour" , and by his might he will judge God`s holy ones and so establish a righteous kingdom, as it is written about him in the Songs of David;"

Ps. 82;1 Scripture also says about him; "Over it take your seat in the highest heaven; A divine being will judge the peoples"

Ps. 7;7 Concerning what scripture says; "How long willyou judge unjustly , and show partiality with the wicked? Selah"

Ps. 82;2, the interpretation applies to Belial and the spirits predestined to him, because all of them have rebelled, turning from God`s precepts and so becoming utterly wicked. Therefore Melchizedek will thoroughly prosecute the vengeance required by God`s statutes. Also, he will deliver all the captives from the power of Belial, and from the power of all the spirits destined to him. Allied with him will be all the righteous divine beings"

JUSTIN MARTYR (Dialogue with Trypho) ponts out that, Melchizedek was not circumcised (Dial 19) and 33). This statement is based on traditions of the day and Justin never cites Hebrews.

TERTULLIAN (polemic agains the Mosaic Law) says that later rabbinic tradition ('Abot R. Nat. 1.12) says he was born circumcised.

Here are a few of our other books are also available for you"

"Apostolic Guidelines to the Prophetic" How to release the prophetic and be safe!

"40 Day Focus on Prosperity" A 40 day study on Biblical prosperity.

"From Enmity to Equality" A comprehensive & scholarly study on women and Christianity

"Whole & Holy" Imparting a passionate longing for Christ-like image and likeness.

"Understanding Headship" A booklet concerning the accurate concepts of headship.

"Finding Wisdom" A book describing how to achieve personal fulfillment.

"Connecting" How to apprehend spiritual realities.

"Why I Speak in Tongues!" A practical book on speaking in tongues.

"Angel's Friends & Curriculum" A Children's book and curriculum on gender and racial equality.

"Melchizedek King Priest" One of the most important studies you will ever undertake to reign in life with ever-increasing dominion.

"Finding Health to Fulfill Your Destiny" A journey into the world of disease-preventing nutrition.

Please go to http://kluane.com and sign up for my monthly newsletter, Rightly Dividing – and also Check out "The School of the Apostles!"
Dr. Kluane - SWORD, P.O.Box 941933, Atlanta, GA 31141

Made in the USA
Columbia, SC
24 May 2020